The Joy of
MATURE
SEX

and
How to Be a
Better Lover

William Campbell Douglass, MD

Rhino Publishing, S.A.

The Joy of
MATURE
SEX

Copyright © 1995, 2003
by
William Campbell Douglass, MD

ISBN 9962-636-48-5

Cover illustration by
Alex Manyoma (alex@3dcity.com)

Please, visit Rhino's website for other publications from
Dr. William Campbell Douglass
www.rhinopublish.com

Dr. Douglass' "Real Health" alternative medical
newsletter is available at www.realhealthnews.com

RHINO PUBLISHING, S.A.
World Trade Center
Panama, Republic of Panama
Voicemail/Fax
International: + 416-352-5126
North America: 888-317-6767

Table of Contents

Introduction
We're So Confused! 5

Chapter 1
Love and Sexuality for Life 9

Chapter 2
The New Eroticism and the New Love 19

Chapter 3
Aging Can Be Delayed 29

Chapter 4
Prescription Medications and
Other Dangers to Your Sex Life 43

Chapter 5
A Few Tricks of the Trade
for Men (and Women) 57

Chapter 6
Men's Health: The Prostate and Beyond 67

Chapter 7
Enhancing Female Sexual
Response — Naturally ....

Conclusion
Secrets of the Heart 93

Other Books by
William Campbell Douglass, MD

- *Add 10 Years To Your Life*
- *Aids And Biological Warfare*
- *Bad Medicine*
- *Color Me Healthy*
- *Dangerous Legal Drugs: The Poisons In Your Medicine Chest*
- *Dr. Douglass Complete Guide To Better Vision*
- *Eat Your Cholesterol! -- Meat, Milk, And Butter -- And Live Longer*
- *Grandma Bell's A To Z Guide To Healing*
- *Hormone Replacement Therapies: Astonishing Results For Men And Women.*
- *Hydrogen Peroxide - Medical Miracle*
- *Into The Light - Tomorrow's Medicine Today*
- *Lethal Injections - Why Immunizations Don't Work*
- *Painful Dilemma -- Patients In Pain -- People In Prison*
- *Prostate Problems: Safe, Simple Effective Relief*
- *St. Petersburg Nights*
- *Stop Aging Or Slow The Process: Exercise With Oxygen Therapy*
- *The Eagle's Feather*
- *The Joy Of Mature Sex And How To Be A Better Lover...*
- *The Smoker's Paradox: The Health Benefits Of Tobacco*

Introduction

We're So Confused!

To be quite honest, we don't really know much about human sex. If fact, most of us seem downright confused about it.

If you don't believe me, just look at corporate America. Every office in this great country is filled with tension between the sexes. You really can't appreciate this unless you've experienced it. It's a mess!

The report you are about to read is not a morality book, nor is it politically correct. It's simply a frank discussion on a subject that most people find interesting, but very confusing. In trying to sort out many of the myths and misunderstandings about sex, I have attempted to put some humor into the subject of sex. It lends itself to humor and, of course, to pathos as well.

I also think you should know up front, I admit to a certain bias in that I am a flaming heterosexual. If you are a flamer of another sort, then you might not get much out of this report. But I may be wrong about that, as I don't understand other "alternatives," as they are called. Men and women seem to go together to me. They may not always get *along*, but they go together in a natural and a biological sense.

If you are interested in free love and total licentious-ness, you need to visit the Bonobos chimps in Zaire. They can teach you a thing or two. The popular press implies that what the Bonobos do, we should do, and that we have "lost" this "freedom" through evolution. But I'm not sure you would want to do all the things the Bonobos do.

Rabbits aren't as perverted as the Bonobos but, as you have probably heard, they are enthusiastic about sex. It was reported in the September 15, 1994 issue of the *Economist,* not your basic sex magazine, that a British re-tired couple started legal action against their neighbors whose rabbits were keeping them awake at night. The rabbits were making "persistent scratching, thumping, and banging noises" — just your routine rabbit sex orgy, but some people just don't appreciate romance.

Among humans, the Swedes originated the do-it-any-time-anywhere-in-any-way-you-like philosophy and what we used to call "free love." Then America took over as the depravity capital of the world (with the VD rate and bastardy stats to prove it), but now we are losing the sex-obsession race to the Germans, You just can't keep those Germans down.

In Germany, from one end to the other, the singles have embraced "sex supermarkets." You put your ad in the paper describing what you want and what you give; the ad is numbered and you go to the disco sex super-market with your number on your shirt, buttocks, or wherever else is appropriate. Get on the dance floor and do your boogie — and look for your meat.

On German TV, there is pornography every night, a talk show on sex or a documentary on the latest trends in sadomasochism or group sex. *Stern* magazine reported (approvingly): "In the era of solitary lust, of sadomasochism, of telephone orgasm, latex lust, and cybersex, ever more people are looking for the superkick.

"Sex has become the most frequent talk show theme, with exhibitionists, child molesters, nymphomaniacs, masochists, and frustrated housewives discussing masturbation, fake orgasms, and sex with the family dog...." It seems that everyone in Germany below the age of 40 is striving for their black belt in sex. The Germans have become sex-obsessed. I call it barbarian.

In the U.S. we are behind in the Bonobo sweepstakes, but I have confidence in America — we'll catch up. When it comes to depravity, we whipped Sweden and we can whip Germany. Never count *us* out of the arms race, or the legs race either.

Humans are very confused about what makes good sex. But I believe humans have more to offer each other than this total licentiousness common among animals. I sometimes make light of the subject of sex, but don't lose sight of the fact that Judeo-Christian morality has been an integral part of the success story of the United States of America. Humor when discussing sex is fine, but don't interpret it as a negation of self-control, Western moral values, and scientific fact. If you do, you're likely to have an unfulfilling and possibly nonexistent sex life as you approach the Golden Years. We're talking about mature sex. The kind of sex that made this country great.

Chapter 1

Love and Sexuality for Life

If asked what's the one thing men and women can do to extend and to improve the quality of life, I would unhesitatingly say love and sex. Actually, that's *two* things because they aren't the same. Being rich definitely helps (I am told), but it too is not enough by itself.

Combined, love and sex offer the human male and female reason to live. And while it is certainly possible to live without one or both of the components, a lifelong love and continued sexual interest can and will keep you young and energetic. Your frame of mind will improve and if the mind improves the body will follow. Some people, especially men, think making money is the reason for living. This type of person never experiences sexual satisfaction and spends large amounts of time and money buying "love."

I've seen men and women literally regenerate themselves — take years off their appearance and add years to their lives — by finding someone who fulfills their emotional and physical desires.

Unfortunately, too many people in America think love and sex are for the young alone. Ask most young people in this country what they think about older couples and sex, and, after the obligatory groan and grimace, they'll tell you that men and women over age 50 don't have sex at all. Our youth culture has conditioned both young and old to think of the over-50 set as nonsexual.

In writing on sex, we have gone from one extreme to the other in the past 40 years. Now it's all out there in graphic detail and you don't have to go to a sleazy storefront decorated with blinking lights to get it either — your local book store will do. In today's more permissive environment we can discuss sex more openly than we could just 40 years ago, so we can attempt to correct these misperceptions without risking a jail sentence.

Everyone was so uptight about sex in 1953, for example, that a book entitled *Curious Customs of Sex and Marriage* by George Scott was limited to a printing of 975 copies. The book was numbered and restricted in sales to "Anthropologists, Ethnologists, Psychologists, Sociologists, the Clergy, and Members of the Medical and Legal Professions." Presumably, other less moral and less stable folk, such as bankers, accountants, salespersons, politicians (probably right there), nuclear physicists, chemists, architects, and the "lowly" housewives wouldn't be able to handle the steamy contents. Maybe they would go off panting to the nearest brothel for sexual release, thus destroying the family, the church, and the radio soap operas.

I got my contraband copy from a used book store in Vancouver and dashed back to my hotel, got out my flashlight and turned out the overhead light. Boy, was I disappointed. The only thing sexy about the book was the title. Here's the first sentence: "The facile critical evaluation of past events ... so often and so increasingly covers blatant ignorance with a thin veneer of neo-sophisticated pseudo-pantologism." Are you still with me?

But on the next page it gets more exciting as we are told that the young female Lacedemonians (I don't know where Lacedemonia is) drag young bachelors around an altar and beat them with sticks. Now this is probably a good idea given young men's disinclination to matrimony, but it's not exactly pornographic reportage.

Now having thoroughly denigrated the book and saving you a fruitless trip to Vancouver, I must say the first page of the first chapter was worth the two quid the book cost me. It's about courtship and bares the charade that it usually is:

"It is a time when the courtier and the courted, owing to the very fact of being in love, are in no state to arrive at any actual or realistic valuation of each other. In many cases both parties are infatuated, and it is quite impossible for the cold light of reason to enter into the matter at all.

"The courting period is inevitably a time of make-believe ... the whole period that elapses before marriage is punctuated with subterfuge, pretense, evasion, repression, and simulation. For no period of courtship, however protracted it may be, and however close the relationship between the engaged parties, can prove as revealing as one single week of actual marriage."

I wish someone had told *me* that. Well, they probably did, but who listens?

Back to the over-50 thing. This national delusion that men over 50 don't make it sexually causes some men and women to think they aren't supposed to enjoy a sexual, loving relationship after they reach middle age. If over 50 means no sex or minimal sex, what's the use of taking vitamins and minerals to stay energetic? What's the sense of staying healthy and active, of looking good and feeling good, if sexuality disappears from your life? It's true that sex isn't the most important thing in the world (after the age of 30), but why give up a good thing with someone you love? You don't need to be the King of the Beasts (a male lion can have sex 85 times in a 24-hour period), but a little sex in your life is a good thing between two loving partners.

Love and sex are God's gifts to us all — and those gifts need not be depleted. Whether you're 20 or 80, love and sex can play a central role in your life. I think it's time for the 50-plus generation to bring its sexuality out of the closet, so to speak. It's time for America and it's aging population to admit to the joy of sex. It's time for couples to share their love and to demonstrate to themselves that love and sex are alive and well and important no matter what the age.

Confronting Your Fears and Culture's Stereotypes

Beginning in our 40s, we are all faced with one of life's greatest fears: losing our ability to attract the opposite sex. From puberty until middle age, whether we like to admit it or not, much of our time is focused on attracting the opposite sex. Even if we're happily married, we all want to know that we are attractive. This builds our self-esteem and there's certainly nothing wrong with that.

But American society places undue emphasis on sexual attractiveness — how else do you explain blond bimbos as television newscasters? Face it, their jobs depend upon how well they look, not on how well they read or even, God forbid, understand what they read.

So, with this cultural emphasis on sex and looks, and with much of our self-esteem built on how we look, very suddenly we find ourselves a little past 40 and feeling less than sexy.

How many times have you seen the balding executive driving the newest, fastest little red sports car? (I have a yellow one.) How often do we see the 40-year-old housewife suddenly raise her hemline up to her gluteal fold? This is an all too natural response to a perceived loss of sexual attractiveness. In short, I can't attract a woman (a man), but maybe my car (sexy hemline) can.

And as we face our 40s, both men and women, but particularly men, begin to wonder if they'll be able to maintain their current level of sexuality. Men worry about impotence; women worry about a loss of sexual attractiveness.

Both fears, and indeed the fear of lessened sexual attractiveness, are often exaggerated. Sex is not for the young only; while the frequency of sex may change — in some cases it may not — the quality of sex does not have to decline. Let me repeat that: the quality of sex does not have to decline with age. The belief in declining sexual enjoyment is the result of a youth and Puritan-based culture that sees middle-aged sex as crude, disgusting, and vaguely immoral.

Don't believe that sex is less important in mid-life than it was in your 20s, or that sex is meant for the young only. Sex is for the young at heart and having sex keeps you young at heart, provided love and monogamy are a major part of your sexual activities.

Remember, in this day of AIDS I am not recommending that you begin dalliances with everyone whom you find attractive. I am asking you to throw away any taboos you may have about sex and middle age, and to forget your unfounded fears of impotence, frigidity, menopause, declining attractiveness, and failure to have a climax. (That happens sometimes, but there is always next time.)

I advocate sex between men and women as a vital part of their loving relationship. Sex keeps you healthy; sex keeps you young; sex helps keep your relationship alive. It's as simple as that.

Sex isn't a cure-all, nor will I tell you that sex in your 40s and 50s is not sometimes fraught with problems. Yes, there are physical changes. Couple these changes with the emotional roller coaster both men and women can exhibit in mid-life, and you can easily see that maintaining a healthy sex life is no longer as simple as letting your raging adolescent hormones do the work. (Did you know that the average teenager sleeps with a *full erection,* according to a researcher at Boston University, for two to three hours a night? I don't know how he discovered that.)

In mid-life, often our concerns are with making a living, providing for our children, fulfilling our responsibilities to work, to our church, and to our community. It's often common in mid-life — and, unfortunately, the pace of American life compounds this problem — to feel tired and exhausted at day's end. The combination of work and stress and family can and often do make sex impossible. There's not enough energy and emotional commitment to go around. It's no secret that during mid-life the frequency of divorce rises.

All of the above create problems that eventually find their way into the bedroom. But these problems are not insurmountable. Often, if handled correctly, these everyday problems are only minor distractions. But the key is to first raise the level of importance sex plays in your -life.

If you're tired, for example, forget the golf game, clean the house later, forget the neighbor's party, tell the kids to eat out. These are all relatively unimportant matters that if left unattended can be handled later, or simply ignored.

But you cannot ignore your sex life; you can't handle it later. Place a loving, sexual relationship with your partner at the top of the list. Believe me, if you do so, you'll find that many of your problems related to sex and your relationship itself will disappear.

Take care of your health first. Part of that care involves maintaining and improving your sex life. Once you place a high priority on a fulfilling sex life, the next step is to begin abandoning the culture's negative notions about sex during your 40s, 50s, 60s, and beyond. You don't have to follow the male pattern in the old joke: "You spend the first 25 years making love, the second 25 years making money and the last 25 years making water."

Assumption number one: Sexual desire declines with age. This may be true, but not necessarily so. We are told in so many subtle and not so subtle ways that sexual desire is a downhill ride after 40. It is true that there is a decrease in the frequency of sexual desire in men as they age (and an increase in most women — things are out of sync; I don't know why God did that). But if you find your desire waning, don't accept it as The End. If there is a decline, it may be due to stress, fatigue, a decline in your relationship, or even a physical problem, such as a testosterone deficiency. Sexual decline can be a symptom, not an inevitable "disease," of old age. Cure the underlying problem, and sexuality can continue at any age, at least to some degree.

I didn't feel I was a good physician until I was well past 40 — and I was right. With age came not only wisdom but self-confidence and the ability to reason without the burning passions of my 20s. I got *better* after 40 (in medicine, I mean). Don't let the MTV generation con you into thinking aging equals death and decline. We all die, as the grim reaper has no respect for age. And eventually our physical abilities *will* decline, but that eventuality can well be when we're in our 80s and beyond.

Age brings wisdom to most, and with wisdom often comes a better understanding of relationships and how to sustain and improve them. With improved relationships comes better sex. Logically, then, we can argue that age brings better sex, so begin today to divest yourself of the notion that age means the inevitable end of your sex life.

If you buy into the myths of middle-age decline and sex is only for the young, your life will reflect these beliefs. You become what you believe; your health reflects what you believe. Think you are old and washed up and you are. Think you are loving and sexual and attractive and you will be.

Assumption number two: You can wear out your sex drive and sex organs. With sex it's the classic case of use it or lose it. The more you have sex in all of its natural manifestations, the more you can have sex, and you'll want to have it more often. There's nothing to wear out. *This means within reason,* however. I'm not talking about Johnny Jackrabbit (see The Cowboy Syndrome in Chapter 4 for the lowdown on the super studs).

Not everyone supports this use-it-or-lose-it theory. Some go so far as to say a man should masturbate often if he .doesn't have a partner in order to avoid losing his sexuality. I don't think this has been proven, but I do recommend that men masturbate once a week if they are not in a sexual relationship simply because I think it is a good idea to insure ejaculate production. I can't prove this. I *know* this goes against some religious precepts, but I'm not of the clergy and I'm just reporting what I think.

The Physical Side of Sex and Middle Age

There's no doubt that the aging process brings with it numerous physical changes. But these changes do not necessarily cause a decline in sexual activity, interest, or performance.

If I had to guess the biggest problem middle-aged men and women face when it comes to sex, I would say it's the psychological problems brought about by culture's insistence on sex for the young only. Not to mention the psychology industry's pushing of various psychological theories meant to make us feel somehow bad and uncomfortable about aging. This includes things like the "let's get sensitive" mantra that robs men of their masculinity and leaves women wondering to where their husbands have disappeared.

We have the women's menopause self-help group, the men's prostate self-help group, the sex over 40 group-sharing session, the Robert Ely weekend-in-the-woods-for-men sessions and any number of other self-pity, hand-wringing organizations. I object to these meetings because they take sex and aging — two natural phenomena — and turn them into problems. These "problems" are seen as so severe it takes a group meeting to address them. Talking to our spouse is not enough; we have to meet with other "victims" to discuss the trauma of aging and sex. And, of course, we need the help of a caring psychologist to "guide" us through this difficult time. (I wonder when *he* last had sex.)

Yes we age, and yes we still need a close sexual relationship with our spouse, no matter how old we may be. What we *don't* need is a group of new-age psychologists making our instincts and needs seem unnatural. To have great sex and to maintain that ability throughout your life takes a strong body, a clear mind, and emotional stability. In my experience, a psychologist or a psychiatrist is not the place to look for a clear mind or emotional stability, although there are exceptions.

Trust yourself and your spouse — and ignore just about everything else. Tell Dr. Ruth to shove off; tell your psychologist to get a real job; and tell yourself that you're comfortable about your sexuality and that age has nothing to do with the enjoyment of sex.

Nothing we are going to say in this penultimate (any sex book will always be penultimate because another sex book is always just around the corner) guide to sexual bliss has been proven to be right for everyone. You must remember that there are only two things that are certain in this life, and they are death and tax evasion.

Chapter 2

The New Eroticism and the New Love

"In our rush to reach the genitals, we take the straight and narrow freeway and miss the lavish countryside of the body itself."

I found this quotation in a popular magazine and thought it went to the heart of the matter. Like everything else in this country, we treat sex and love as if they are Olympic events. We're concerned with numbers: how many times do you do it, how long does it take you to do it, how many people have you done it with?

With this emphasis on numbers, we have to keep count of how often we score — and scoring is sexual intercourse. Ultimately, then, why should we bother with caring and sharing and alternative sexual acts that don't involve intercourse? If scoring is the goal, then score we will.

Maybe, and I stress the maybe, the frequency of sex declines as we age. We may make love less, and if we're smart we limit our partner to one. But numbers alone are no indication of quality, sexuality, or love. As we age, I believe that we have a great opportunity to finally overcome the numbers game and develop what I call a new perspective on eroticism and love.

Let me say this: If you are in your 40s, 50s, or 60s and you continue to play the numbers game, you are setting yourself up for failure. When it comes to sheer numbers, the young win every time. But if you develop a new look at eroticism and love — one that eliminates numbers and concentrates on quality and emotional fulfillment — sex may improve, not decline, with age.

You don't believe me about the age thing? In January 1994, in Odessa, Texas, there was a very strange killing, done in "self-defense." A 90-year-old woman gave her 91-year-old husband a resounding blow to the head with her cane after he became "too boisterous" in his demand for sex. That was the last foreplay for this progressive gentleman. He was dead on arrival at the hospital, but it was decided not to prosecute the unwilling lady. So you see? Anything is possible.

My idea of eroticism and love includes less intercourse and more touching; less penetration and more contemplation; less orgasm and more fulfillment. If you would like to try this new eroticism right now, here's a simple exercise for you and your mate.

First, set the mood. That is, establish the proper setting by dimming the lights (candles are great), tuning into the proper music or sounds, and establishing a quiet calm between you and your partner.

Now remove your clothes and sit back to back with your partner. Feel each other's heartbeat — you can feel the pulsing through your back, almost as if it was in the backbone. Just sit and breathe together.

After a few minutes of quiet, turn face to face. Keep still and let the feeling of each other wash over you.

Continue to breathe together — and resist the urge to reach for the genitals. Stay calm, yet sexually charged.

After several minutes of face to face contact, then and only then let things happen naturally. Perhaps intercourse will be the result, but perhaps not. Maybe you and your partner will just hold each other. That's fine. Intercourse isn't necessary — no one is keeping score and the goal isn't to "score." For the first time in a long time allow yourselves to do whatever comes naturally.

This exercise demonstrates what I call the new eroticism. And I believe you'll find this new attitude and new method of making love superior to youthful, Olympic-style lovemaking.

I think you can see that my view of eroticism is centered on touch. That's why I was so interested in the quote about rushing to the genitals. In our rush to consummate the act we barely touch each other!

As we age, we need more touching, not less. In this age when we are afraid to touch each other (and with good reason; things like AIDS, TB, and a new breed of contagious diseases have made us hands-off), the need for touch has reached epidemic proportions. I contend that a return to touching is the very best way for those 40 years old and beyond to reestablish contact with partners, and to reinstall the spark of sexual attraction.

And those of you in monogamous relationships have the great advantage of being able to explore touch to its fullest. Without the fear of AIDS, you can explore each other's bodies with no limit: no condoms, no creams, no fear.

Touch brings intimacy; sex does not. Strive to achieve intimacy through touch. In the long run, sexual fulfillment will be greater. And I promise you'll feel closer to your partner than you have in years. Try some sensual massage, slow your lovemaking down, and concentrate on one part of your partner's anatomy — and not the genitals.

What may amaze you is that it is possible to achieve orgasm without genital stimulation. If you know your body, and take the time to understand your partner's body, there is no limit to the joys of sex and love.

Sexual intercourse is easy; it takes very little effort. Building an erotic relationship with your partner takes time and caring. As we age, time and caring are the two things we need most. As our 91-year-old amorata from Odessa, Texas, found out late in life, that's important, especially to women.

Sexual Myths

I've already touched on a couple of common misconceptions about sex, but I'm convinced the myths surrounding sex so cloud our minds that real sexual fulfillment is difficult to achieve for most of us. What's worse, combine these sexual myths with the myths of aging, and it's a wonder to me that middle-aged American couples have any satisfying sex at all.

The way we think about sex, without doubt, affects the way we feel about this gift. So let's clear the air, if we can, and look at some of the most damaging myths about sex.

1. Sex is shameful: I don't think anybody really believes this absolutely. Even the most strict Christian church will tell you that sex between married partners is wonderful — a gift from God. There's nothing wrong with having sex or wanting sex.

Our bodies are built to respond to love and attention, and sex is part of that response. Sex between unmarried couples? That's up to your beliefs. Sex between men or sex between women — that is clearly an abomination; most states have laws against such conduct.

But remember this: if you have a loving relationship, sex is not only "permitted," I think it should be encouraged; preferably, of course, in the married state.

2. Sex is for having children: This goes back to some dark-age religious beliefs. First of all, sex is more than intercourse. Much of what men and women do for each other will not result in pregnancy; yet it is part of the marriage chamber, so it cannot be wrong — and it's *still* sex.

And if sex were just for procreation, wouldn't it make sense that human sexual response would be more like an animal's, with the females coming into season once or twice a year? The human male and female can copulate at any time. God must have had sex for loving and caring in mind.

3. Sex involves the genitals: I've addressed this point already, but let me repeat it. If your sexual encounters are a rush to the genitals, you are cheating both you and your partner out of some very wonderful, loving encounters. One goal of sex is intimacy with your partner. There are 1,001 ways to reach this intimacy through erotic touch and erotic talk. Don't limit yourself to intercourse.

4. The key is performance: No! The keys are enjoyment, fun, caring, and sharing. If you keep score, you lose! I'll discuss this in greater detail in a minute.

5. There's one right way to make love: No! There may be some wrong ways, but there is no single right way. If you and your partner enjoy something, then that

something is right for you. By letting some expert tell you there's a right way, you are opening yourself up to criticism and more good, old-fashioned guilt! Do what's right for both you and your partner. You can't really go wrong.

6. The quality of sex depends upon your partner's abilities: Not really. Sex is a two-way street. Like everything in this life, from financial goals to health care, you are responsible for yourself. That doesn't mean you ignore your partner; it means that you take responsibility. Isn't this the mature approach to lovemaking?

7. Sex must end in orgasm: No! If orgasm were the goal, the sex act for men would be about 20 seconds; for women, a little longer. Sexual fulfillment means just that, a fulfilling encounter with the person you love. Orgasm doesn't equal fulfillment. If it did, masturbation would be the sex method of choice.

Sexual fulfillment can involve orgasm, but it doesn't have to. If you believe it does, you are putting unnecessary pressure on yourself, and limiting the number of sexual activities you can enjoy.

8. Sex follows a pattern: Sometimes yes, but not usually. Sure you and your partner may fall into a comfortable pattern, but this, too, will change and evolve. The couples who maintain their sexual spirit well into their third and fourth decades of marriage will tell you that physical needs change. What once stimulated them no longer does.

In a real sense, then, sex is constant experimentation. Isn't that wonderful news? You can't ever learn it all and you can't ever get it perfect because it changes. There's no need for multiple partners when one partner can have multiple needs.

Seven Things You Can Do Right Now to Start Enjoying Sex More Than Ever

I'm not one to follow the philosophies of the East, nor do I fall for that new-age pretension about mystical sexual experiences, the Kama Sutra, and the like. But while researching this book, I came across a book entitled "The Art of Sexual Ecstasy." I don't recommend the book, unless you want to learn Buddhist names for your body parts. But I did enjoy one small section that dealt with attitude.

After reading it, I realized that a quick change in mind-set may be just what many adults need to increase their sexual enjoyment almost immediately. With a bit of poetic license, I share these ideas with you.

1. Learn Self-Love: It's the oldest saying in the world, "You can't love others until you love yourself." That goes double for enjoying sex. If you love yourself, you will want to please yourself, and sex is a part of that pleasure. If you love yourself, you'll have more love to share, and unequivocally, more love means better sex. And the more you love yourself, the more love you will attract from your partner. It's a win-win situation. Start by taking a new look at yourself, and a new sexual power will emerge. But be warned, don't love yourself so much that you're not willing to give yourself away (see number 7 on the next page). That's selfishness and breeds a poor love life.

2. Forget Guilt: I'll say it again: You're an adult and you have the right to enjoy adult activities. That means having sex with your partner. Eliminate the guilt. Don't let voices from your past interfere with the present.

3. Cultivate Pleasure: We spend so much time working, raising children, and doing our civic duty, that we

Americans have little time for real pleasure. Consider, sex is a totally pleasurable experience, and a gift of pleasure you can give to yourself and your mate. Take the time to enjoy your body and your loving relationship with your mate. Work is fine; but pleasure is essential to life.

4. Be Spontaneous: I know it's hard with the kids and work, but you can't let your life fall into too much of a pattern. That goes for your sex life, too. For one evening, be spontaneous with your spouse. Forget the planning, have dinner, see a movie, spend time together just because you want to. Throw away the clock and the calendar and enjoy yourself. If sex happens to be a part of that spontaneous evening, I'll bet it will be wonderful.

5. Relax: If that means spending a few minutes each day praying or meditating or walking, whatever, you must relax. To enjoy a long life, relaxation is essential. To enjoy a long life of wonderful sex, relaxation must be a part of your life. We'll discuss the importance of this in greater detail in the next chapter.

6. Forget Goals: I mean sexual goals. Forget the number, the time, and the frequency of orgasms. Sex is not a game. There is no score, no clock, no winners and losers. If you want to take up a sport, try tennis. If you want to develop a deeper relationship with your spouse, try sex without goals.

7. Surrender: Give yourself totally to your partner. Freely surrender to your mate and to whatever feelings arise during sex. Let yourself go. The marriage bed, or floor, or sofa, is the one place where you can let yourself go totally free without embarrassment and without consequences. For this reason alone, good sex is the equivalent of good health.

As you know if you are a steady reader of my newsletters, I do not think psychologists are equipped to tell us how to run our lives. They don't know any more about sex, love, and the lack of both than the rest of us. What they are taught in their "training" is a distillation of the opinions of professors who are themselves often in need of help.

The one exception to this general "prejudice" of mine is Dr. Bernie Zilbergeld, who is a Ph.D. psychologist with a vast amount of common sense. Dr. Zilbergeld says: "Popular culture has done a convincing job of ignoring married sex, or showing that it is nothing to get excited about; ... we see lots of sex in new relationships. Is the sex of long-term relationships really so bad?

"Clearly for most people, sexually fulfilling relationships are the products of time, familiarity, and a major commitment in effort and cooperation." (From: *Good Health Report*, May 1993.)

Now let me add one more thing you can do to increase your sexual fulfillment: *Add some fun into your love!*

Love making isn't serious business — it's pleasure and it should be fun. Be playful, experiment, but most of all, throw away your inhibitions.

Having given you a pep talk on surefire great sex, let's now turn the coin over and look at life and love *without* sex. If you're 20, and unmarried, you probably don't think that's possible.

Some couples are insufferable and others are inseparable. If you are on another collision course for a "quickie" romance, and I consider anything less than a year definitely a quickie, then what follows probably won't interest you.

Zsa Zsa Gabor, speaking to a meeting of mostly males, said: "I don't know anything about sex. I've always been married." It may surprise you to learn that many Americans didn't find that remark to be at all startling. The National Survey of Sexual Attitudes found that only 16 percent of women and 17 percent of men thought that sex was the most important part of a relationship.

Laura Marcus, reporting in *Options* magazine, told the story of Fiona and Richard. They are in their 30s and stopped having sex after six years of marriage and haven't had sex in four years. They are perfectly happy and as close as ever. "We had a good sex life once," Fiona said. "But sex belongs to a different phase — we're not interested."

Marcus reported another case where the mother of one of the spouses became upset and recommended "counseling" when the wife said she and her husband no longer had sex. Counseling for what, the daughter retorted. "We're happy. We have a marvelous time, a great social life, and we're very close."

Sex starts a lot of relationships, but many long-lastrng couplings have little sex and often none at all. A new study from the University of Chicago, called the Social Organization of Sexuality, explodes many of the myths about sex in America. Of married couples interviewed, 60 percent had sex a few times a month, a few times a year, or never. So it's hardly rare or abnormal for couples to have little or no sex. It was perhaps more surprising that of the "swinging singles," the ones who are supposed to be doing it all the time, 77 *percent* had sex only a few times a month, a few times a year, or never.

Chapter 3

Aging Can Be Delayed

I believe it will soon be possible for most people to live to the age of 100 and beyond. Best of all, during those 100 years we'll be able to live full, energetic lives right up to the very end. Almost daily, researchers are discovering that the aging process can be slowed. That's good news for all of us.

Part of this research involves sex and love. It appears that a healthy sex life is one that goes well past the 50s and 60s and into the 70s, 80s, and beyond.

Sex when you're in your 80s? There's nothing wrong with that. (Unless you get too forceful with your 90-year-old wife; then you get your brains bashed out.) And, in fact, research shows that a healthy sex life is one indicator of a long life. (Or is it the other way around?)

Many of you may find all of this hard to believe, but that's only because most of us harbor several misconceptions about aging.

If you understand the aging process, you'll have less fear. And you certainly won't let anyone tell you that sexual fulfillment decreases with age — it does with most people, but it doesn't have to. Note that I said *fulfillment*, not frequency.

First, let's discuss the physical facts of aging. The body will decline after age 40, but that decline does not necessarily mean an end to sex; a change, but not the end.

For example, contrary to popular belief, there's no evidence that your heart's ability to pump decreases with age. Provided your heart is not diseased, the heart of a 70-year-old beats just about as strongly as that of a 40-year-old. It will not be able to sustain the same degree of *intense exercise* as a man of 40, but with intelligent use of the powers that remain, the performance can be as satisfactory as that of a 40-year-old. Maybe better. (You don't get to 70 without learning *something?*)

Lung capacity does decrease with age. You may notice a slight decline when you reach your 60th year, but even that isn't inevitable. And the slight decline in no way affects your ability to work, play, or make love — if you use your remaining capacity judiciously. The best way to compensate for a diminished cardiopulmonary reserve is to have your partner take the top position. As the climax approaches, you can roll over and demonstrate your tiger/bull/sex-dog magnificence.

Like men and women of all ages, the range of sexual activity among older Americans is wide. It shouldn't surprise you to learn that some 70-year-olds make love more frequently than their 35-year-old counterparts who are rushing to cut a path through corporate America.

The ability to have sex in your 60s and 70s has more to do with your state of mind than with your physical condition. Here's the bottom line: if you think you're sexy, you probably are.

Finally, it's just not true that our mental abilities decline with age. Yes, brain cells die, but that's a natural phenomenon as you age. I've seen no studies that indicate the normal process of dying brain cells means declining brain *function*. This is because your years of experience, and practicing the routines of life, compensate for the lost cells. Brain cells will not replace the judgment gained through the experiences, and mistakes, of life.

What does cause a decline in mental ability is very much . the same factor relating to a decline in sexual activity: use it or lose it. If the brain remains active, stimulated with thoughts and challenging activities, it remains youthful. In short, mental exercise is as essential as physical exercise. Not all gerontologists agree with that.

Of course, you understand that all bets are off if you don't take care of yourself. I've seen some unhealthy 30-year-old men who couldn't make love under any circumstances, even with the latest fashion sex goddess. Stay healthy and active, and I can almost guarantee that your sex life will remain as satisfying as ever.

So let me put the final myth to rest: *Aging is not a disease.* Aging is a natural process that does not have to include senility, incapacity, and asexuality, at least not until you reach a *really* old age, say 100 or so.

I argue that we need to develop a new image of aging: One that doesn't frighten people into a lifeless and futile contemplation of the hereafter. By now, you should have made up your mind about that. So *stay busy* and enjoy your last decade or so, with or without sex. Recently, I read yet another report of a Frenchman in his 80s who fathered a child. I guess no one ever told him that he would lose his sex drive. It's a wise man who knows his father.

Don't be frightened into an early, sexless old age. As one popular song says, "If you never slow down, you never grow old."

This admonition applies doubly for sex and love. The more sexually active you stay, the more sexy you'll be. And sexual activity has the added benefits of keeping you physically fit and psychologically healthy. I can think of no better way to stay active than to stay sexually active.

A fulfilling sex life not only stimulates your body, it stimulates your mind. Am I saying sex can help defeat senility? I don't know, but you can have fun finding out.

Some Advice for Men

The media have told us, in no uncertain terms, that once we're into our 40s, sex is downhill. We can't perform as well as young men, we're not as attractive as younger men, and our potency will continue to decline until — when we reach our late 50s — we will be almost non-sexual.

Like women and menopause, men in their 40s face dozens of unfounded fears, usually categorized by the dreaded "mid-life" crisis.

Yes, there are physical changes that occur as men age, but these changes do not adversely affect sexuality or the ability to have sex in most men. But if you are silly enough to buy into the myth of the impotent middle-aged male, then you may have some problems.

As men age, it may take a little longer to achieve an erection. This slightly slowed response is natural, yet it frightens men because they see it as an indicator of declining sexual ability. Well, it *is* a sign of decline, but it doesn't mean it's all over. This slowed response is not important unless you *make* it important. It does not indicate the beginning of impotence nor does it mean that sexual desire is waning. It means only that you are aging naturally and (we hope) gracefully. Instead of instant erection, it now takes a minute or two. That's meaningless in the grand scheme of things, unless you think sex is supposed to be completed in a matter of minutes. (A bull does it in about 30 seconds.) In fact, this slowed response means that men need foreplay, just as women do. This can be a blessing to your partner and to you. Enjoy the extra time; be creative and relax.

As men reach their late 50s and early 60s, it's possible that the erection may not be as hard or as large. But once fully excited, the erection will most likely be hard and steady. Many men find that manual stimulation by their partner is needed to gain a full erection.

As a man ages, there's likely to be a reduction in the amount of seminal fluid, but this, too, is normal. And, in fact, it may be a bonus. Less seminal fluid usually means that men can delay ejaculation for a longer period of time. Again, this benefits both partners. It's common for the length of lovemaking to increase as men age. There's absolutely nothing wrong with that.

Some men worry that their orgasms become less powerful with age. In some cases, this may be true, but less powerful does not mean less enjoyable. Men may also notice that it takes longer to have another erection after orgasm. As teenagers, it may take a matter of minutes after orgasm; in their 40s, many men find it takes a matter of hours. In your 70s it may take a few days or weeks. But this increase in time in no way reflects a loss in sexuality — you don't have to have sex every day and neither does your wife. (Unless you have a 19-year-old "trophy bride." Then you have a problem of your own making and you definitely need a penile prosthesis and a bedside cardiologist.)

Like I said in the previous chapter, lovemaking does not always have to involve ejaculation. As we age, both men and women realize that there are other parts to making love other than orgasm. Don't limit your lovemaking only to those times when ejaculation is possible. Experiment, have fun; there's lots to do once the pressure of performance is lifted. Did you hear the joke about the 90-year-old couple who were still madly in love? At night, as soon as the light was turned off, he would place his hand gently on hers and they would fall into a blissful sleep. One night, as he placed his hand on her hand, she carefully drew it away and said: "Not tonight, Darling, I have a headache."

If all this talk on sex is just exhausting you, then maybe you should try a tree marriage. No, I'm not nuts; it's the Hindus who are strange. Since most Hindus think the unmarried state is downright unpatriotic, abnormal, and obnoxious, the only way out for the reluctant young man is to marry a tree. A tree has a spirit, the Hindus say, and that is what you are marrying.

There are advantages to marrying a tree. They don't shop, they don't talk back and they won't run away with a rock star. There are disadvantages to this cross marrying, but if you don't like sex maybe it's the answer for you. (Try an oak, a little messy but they provide good shade and smell nice.)

Maintaining Sexual Fitness

If you have your health, you have everything. That saying goes double for an active, fulfilling sex life. If you can maintain your health, you can have a wonderful sex life well into your 70s and 80s.

My advice is simple. First, keep your weight down. If you keep your weight down, you'll maintain your attractiveness and your ability to have sex on a regular basis. Keeping your weight down is also the best natural way to lower your blood pressure, at least that's the popular medical opinion. I'm not sure it's completely valid, but low blood pressure probably does mean a healthier heart. If it's true, it will keep you away from sex-ruining blood-pressure medication. I'm not recommending here that you become skinny — "pleasingly plump" is OK. There's no point in fighting Mother Nature; you're not going to change mutton into lamb.

Exercise Regularly

A regular exercise program will improve how you look, how you feel about yourself, and how well your body will function sexually. Exercise has no drawbacks unless you go overboard and exercise to the point of exhaustion. (When you're tired, sex is the first thing to suffer.)

Forget the health club and take a walk.

Your exercise plan should include a two to three mile walk each day, or every other day. The pace of the walk is unimportant. Walk as fast as you comfortably can. Walking keeps your heart healthy and it keeps your body limber — again, two things necessary for great sex.

If you can walk for 30 to 60 minutes each day, you'll notice a rapid increase in your stamina and strength.

Walking reduces stress, and that can increase your libido. And you'll look better — that's not bad when it comes to sexuality.

Also, I heartily recommend any exercise program that includes swimming. Swimming is low impact, which is ideal if you have arthritis. And swimming is a total body experience. Your upper and lower body get a real workout. You can swim at your own pace; indoor pools even remove the problem of bad weather.

No matter what your age, a little exercise will do you good; just don't overdo it. Too much of a good thing, even great sex, is not good for you.

How About the Kegel?

Many sex manuals recommend that both men and women do the Kegel exercise each day. All women who have gone to prenatal classes know about the Kegel. It's a squeezing exercise meant to improve the tone of pelvic muscles. Recently, research has shown that the Kegel can benefit both men and women.

Here's how to do the Kegel. You can be standing or sitting; it doesn't matter. Just be comfortable.

The exercise involves squeezing and releasing the muscles in your pelvic region. How do you know which muscles to exercise? The muscles you're trying to exercise are those that you use when you are trying to stop yourself from urinating. Those are the muscles that help to control the vaginal walls in women and the erection in men. By squeezing these muscles for five seconds, then releasing, you are toning the very muscles that are needed for sex. Start with 20 to 30 contractions, two or three times each day.

In a matter of weeks, women will notice the ability to increase pressure on the penis during intercourse; men will notice more control of their erections, harder erections, and a greater ability to delay ejaculation.

Some women have noticed increased satisfaction by doing the Kegel during intercourse. Try the Kegel. It can't hurt and it can help to maintain muscle tone in the uterus, bladder, and rectum.

Get Some Rest

Great sex takes time, attention, and energy. From the comments of my patients over the years, what's lacking in many relationships is energy. The day in, day out grind of making a living and taking care of the kids just about kills any extra energy we may have for great sex.

But in an odd way, this energy problem is reduced for many older Americans. I've had many patients in the late 50s and early 60s comment to me about how their sex lives have improved with age. These couples are financially more secure than during their younger years; most have raised their children and so the pressures of parenting are gone.

For these couples, then, there's more time for developing a deeper relationship, one that includes more sexual contact. Provided there are no underlying medical problems, there's more energy available for sex. This is especially true on vacations.

So you see, getting older does have its advantages when it comes to sex.

If, however, you are like most Americans, having enough energy at the end of the day for sex is problematical. There may not be a solution to this problem, but I can make a few suggestions.

The amount of energy you have is directly related to how long and how deeply you sleep. As we age, sleep comes less easily. Studies show that older Americans sleep less deeply than do the young. And as we age, there's a greater chance that we will awaken during the night (3:00 a.m. seems to be the magic hour) and thus ruin a good night's sleep.

Take a look at your sleep pattern. If you're sleeping less and find yourself awake for part of the night, it's time to take action. Better sleep means better sex, so it's important that you find ways to improve your sleep.

Avoid sleeping pills! Unless, of course, you want to be groggy all day and ruin your sex life by decreasing your libido.

Naturally, you should avoid caffeine in the evening. If you're having trouble sleeping, I suggest you stop all caffeine intake after 5:00 p.m.

A few years ago, I would have told you to take 1-tryptophan. This is a great calmative and sleep enhancer. But the PDA in its wisdom has banned tryptophan *because someone sold one contaminated batch.*

But there's encouraging news. Recent studies have shown that melatonin can help you to fall asleep faster and stay asleep longer. Many health food stores are now selling the supplement, although some fear another PDA ban. If it works for you, stock up.

There are several types of melatonin supplements available. I recommend the sublingual tablets. Place one tablet under your tongue at bedtime and say good night.

Many of my patients report that sublingual melatonin gives them the best night's sleep they've had in years.

Remember, if you're not sleeping well, you're not rested; if you're not rested, good sex just isn't possible. This is far more true for a man than a woman. Women may disagree with that, but I think it's true.

Nutrients That May Help You Keep Going

Another key to a longer life is proper nutrition. This is really important as we age, since it has been shown that most older Americans are lacking in essential vitamins and minerals. (It may be that as the metabolism slows, we are less able to absorb vital nutrients.)

Proper nutrition is essential for proper mental functioning. An English study showed that almost one-third of patients admitted to a mental hospital were deficient in either vitamin B complex or vitamin C.

Along with traditional vitamin and mineral supplements, here are a few other nutrients to consider taking; ones that can help slow the aging process, and keep you sexually active.

Coenzyme QIO: Coenzyme QIO is nothing short of a miracle when it comes to strengthening the heart and treating certain types of heart failure. For natural physicians, Coenzyme QIO is the preferred method of treatment for heart disease. And Coenzyme QIO helps stimulate the immune system, so it should be used as a preventive. Take 60 mg, once a day.

EPA (eicosapentaenoic acid): EPA is derived from certain fish oils and has been shown to help prevent heart disease. It has also been shown to decrease the possibility of blood clots by making blood less "sticky". Take 360 mg, twice daily.

Garlic: This amazing plant can help fight disease, strengthen your heart, and increase your sexual appetite. As an antiaging nutrient, it has been shown that garlic helps control cholesterol and protects against narrowing of the arteries.

I recommend 600 mg (one-half clove) to 1200 mg (one clove) per day for adults. Studies have shown that garlic's effects in the body are limited over time, particularly the blood-clotting protection of garlic. So to insure constant blood levels of garlic, and thus constant protection, one tablet after each meal and one before bed is the best way to take your garlic (each tablet is about 300 mg).

L-carnitine: This amino acid has been shown to protect against some types of heart disease. It also works to increase the level of HDL — the good cholesterol. Take 250 mg, twice daily.

Lecithin: This dietary supplement has shown a wide range of antiaging abilities. Lecithin helps maintain the proper functioning of the nervous system. I've seen some evidence that lecithin supplementation can help improve memory. Take 1200 mg, twice daily.

Zinc: For men, zinc is a vital element in maintaining the proper functioning of the prostate gland. If there's one nutrient men should take for their reproductive system, it's 25-50 mg of zinc each day.

Proper nutrition also affects your ability to have children. Some people, by the way, have sex for the purpose of having babies. It's not as common as it used to be, but it still happens. If you are interested in this aspect of sex, you might want to consider moving to an organic farm.

A report in an early June 1994 issue of the *Lancet* medical journal indicates that organic farming is not just good for growing healthy vegetables. Scientists in Denmark found that organic farmers, compared to farmers who used pesticides in their food production, have *twice the sperm density* of the pesticide users.

Now, you say, "I don't live on a farm at all so what has this got to do with me?" A good question. I guess I was just trying to make the point that if you want to get pregnant, you should avoid pesticides. (Why did I get into this?) Actually, if pesticides adversely affect your reproductive organs, they will eventually affect your sex life. I strongly recommend that you purchase vegetables that are organically grown. They may be a little more expensive, but worth every penny. Read on for more information about other dangers to your sex life.

Chapter 4

Prescription Medications and Other Dangers to Your Sex Life

Nothing adversely affects male and female sexuality more than prescription medications, including over-the-counter drugs.

There's a vicious cycle at work here. As men and women age, traditional doctors are inclined to offer any number of drugs for a limitless number of real or perceived medical problems. This drugging of the over-40 set causes sexual problems for both partners. In turn, it's another visit to the doctor to help with the sexual dysfunction, it's another round of drugs, and the vicious circle begins.

Unfortunately, so many men and women accept the false beliefs about the inevitable decline of sexuality as we age that the drug-induced reduction in libido or sexual functioning is accepted as "natural." It's sad that thousands of Americans accept a reduced sex life as a matter of course. They don't see how much of their problem is being caused by drugs combined with America's prejudice against any group that's not slim and 20.

Even the AMA admits that 25 *percent of sexual problems in men are caused by doctor-prescribed medications.* This figure may be underestimated, but it indicates that even the AMA understands the problem. In it's typical 19th-century manner, the AMA has a difficult time admitting that women, too, are adversely affected by prescription drugs.

The following drug groups can cause serious problems with male and female sexuality.

Tranquilizers: Why anyone would take any tranquilizer is beyond me. To begin, there are literally dozens of natural remedies that can help you to reduce stress and relax. Believe me, a cup of warm chamomile tea can cut stress almost immediately; B vitamins can help reduce stress; melatonin can help you sleep through the night. The list is endless.

All tranquilizers greatly and adversely affect male sexual function. For many men, it will be impossible to achieve an erection; for others, tranquilizers make it impossible to maintain an erection or to reach orgasm. And tranquilizers can reduce sexual feelings in both men and women.

Antidepressants: Like tranquilizers, even the most backwoods physician knows that antidepressants — all antidepressants — adversely affect sexuality in men and women.

Antihypertensives: For men, these blood-pressure-lowering drugs are not only unnecessary in most cases, but in almost all cases they cause impotence. Some of these pharmaceuticals actually reduce blood flow to the pelvic region. Other antihypertensive medications make it impossible to ejaculate. And sexual interest can be greatly reduced with this class of drugs.

If you have high blood pressure, try a daily regimen of garlic and vitamin E. Add some magnesium and potassium to your diet. A slow walk each day may even help. And all of the above suggestions will not only lower your blood pressure, they will increase your sexuality. But don't just suddenly stop taking medication for hypertension. These drugs are dangerous and sudden cessation can cause sudden death.

Cortisone: I *hate* cortisone. It's the drug most doctors give you when they don't have any idea what to do. A bit of arthritis, have some cortisone. Bad sinuses, try some cortisone. But remember this: every time a man takes cortisone he runs the risk of temporary impotence — and a lot of even worse things. There is a place for cortisone but it's not the cure-all that we once thought — and it's definitely bad for the bedroom.

Alcohol: Get a woman to have a drink or two and she'll be more inclined to have sex. Know what? That's true — to a point. Recent studies have shown that one or two drinks can relax a woman and help to increase her sexual interest. More than one or two, however, and alcohol works on women as a depressant. It decreases sexual response and can inhibit the ability to reach orgasm.

For men, alcohol is a real depressant. It offers no advantages related to sexuality, and it comes with numerous drawbacks. Alcohol can ruin a man's sexual drive and adversely affect his performance. When drinking, erections can be less firm and ejaculation can be impaired.

Alcoholism is the beginning of the end for sexuality. Alcoholism causes liver damage, neurological damage, and circulatory problems. Any one of these problems is enough to stop sexuality in its tracks.

A note for both men and women: As we age, alcohol has a greater effect on our physical and emotional responses. Two or three drinks at age 20 have much less effect than two or three drinks when you're 50, For men over 40, it's best to avoid alcohol for several hours before sexual activity. For women, one or two drinks (beer or wine) an hour before sexual activity may make the experience more pleasurable. If you were around during World War II, you probably heard the expression of our boys overseas: "Candy is dandy, but liquor is quicker."

We now know why liquor is quicker. (I guess scientists will eventually explain everything — except females, of course.) Finnish and Japanese doctors reported in the journal *Nature* that their studies had revealed alcohol causes women to produce more testosterone. And we all know what testosterone does — it disrupts an otherwise peaceful existence. (But it's worth it.)

Prescription Drugs and Men's Sexuality

Impotence strikes such fear in men that one bout of it (and all men will have a time or two when the body does not respond) leads to anxiety, which, in turn, compounds the problem, turning a single episode into a permanent condition. The best way to fight impotence is with calm composure and a bit of information.

Most cases of impotence can be corrected. Unless there's an underlying physical problem, impotence is most likely a one or two-time occurrence that will take care of itself. And it is likely that these natural episodes will occur more frequently as men age. But that's no indication that sexual ability or desire has diminished.

One important fact that most men don't realize is that as men age, they usually need more physical contact before achieving an erection. So, if your erections don't occur as frequently as they once did, don't worry. With a little stimulation, all will be well. Consider this as nothing more than a natural change in your sexual appetite.

I believe there are many causes of impotence. Stress is at an all-time high as the American economy continues to suffer. Men and women work harder for less, and the result is often a level of fatigue that results in impotence for many men. Many times, impotence has nothing to do with sexuality. It has more to do with stress and performance anxiety. But that's just one the many potential causes of impotence.

The Single Most Frequent Cause of Impotence: Prescription Drugs

It may very well be that impotence increases as men age because older men are given more prescription drugs by their doctors. I swear, most people I know in their 50s and 60s are taking enough prescription drugs to start their own pharmacies.

As we age, doctors think it's fine to prescribe drug after drug after drug: drugs for high blood pressure, for insomnia, for anxiety. Most of these drugs adversely affect your prostate, your sexual drive, and your ability to maintain an erection.

Male sexual functioning is fragile enough, without the added problem of prescription and over-the-counter drugs. Something as simple as an antihistamine can wreck an evening's romance.

If you've experienced sudden impotence, the first thing to do is look at the prescription and over-the-counter drugs you are taking. Eliminate as many of these drugs as is safely possible and abstain from all alcohol. I also suggest you read my book *What You Must Know About the Poisons in Your Medicine Chest* (Now available as *Dangerous Legal Drugs* with Rhino Publishing www.rhinopublish.com) I wrote this book particularly for men and women over age 50. It outlines which drugs are dangerous and lists those that can adversely affect sexuality.

Even those over-the-counter drugs that seem benign can irritate the prostate. Foremost among these are antihistamines. In many men, particularly those over age 50, antihistamines play a role in impotence and incontinence. And they adversely affect the prostate and the bladder. What's so insidious about antihistamines is that they are so readily available, and most of us think of them as totally safe. *They're not!*

Drugs that fight hypertension are notorious for causing impotence, as are antidepressants. You shouldn't be taking antidepressants in the first place. Impotence is not supposed to occur "naturally" as you age and may be a sign that you are damaging your system with needless drugs.

Blood-pressure medications present more problems than just impotency. These problems include incontinence, reduced sexual urge and overall energy, and it's an irritation to the prostate (increasing the symptoms of BPH).

Amphetamines, narcotics, even marijuana can also cause impotence. The notion that marijuana somehow makes sex better may work for a 20-year-old, but it's not for you old guys. In fact, pot may make sex impossible. As a simple rule of thumb: most prescription drugs and some over-the-counter drugs have the potential to affect sexuality and the overall condition of your prostate — not to mention the rest of your system. If you suddenly develop symptoms of BPH there's a good chance a medication is involved. It makes good sense that if you begin taking a new medication and symptoms of BPH suddenly occur, chances are the drug is the culprit.

Another Cause of Impotence: Vasectomy

I have always maintained that a man cannot escape harm from this operation any more than a woman can escape harm from a tubal ligation. In both cases a natural channel is being blocked. Where does the sperm go? Where does the blocked egg go and what effect does this blockage have on hormone levels in males and females?

Ben, a merchant banker, had his "snip" 15 years ago. He was relieved when all the "scare stories" about vasectomy being linked to cancer and heart disease died down. It never occurred to Ben, and apparently to his surgeon either, that the vasectomy could be a threat to his manhood. But over the past two years, Ben has been becoming steadily impotent. He found that he could only achieve an erection four times in every 10 tries and, even if he did succeed, he would shrink after penetration. If he got beyond that hurdle, he would usually fail to ejaculate.

Now a study from England supports my view. Dr. Richard Petty, who runs a Well-Man clinic in London, reported on a study of 445 men who complained of impotence. He found a "marked reduction" in testosterone levels when more than 10 years had elapsed since the vasectomy.

Ben was shocked when it was suggested that his vasectomy, done over a decade ago, might be the cause of his impotence. His testosterone level was 15.8 whereas the average for his age is 20. Dr. Petty said: "Men contemplating a vasectomy must take a calculated risk and accept it could have an erosive effect on testosterone levels. I would not have one myself."

Dr. Petty said there is no explanation why testosterone levels go *up* following surgery and then, years later, drop off. "Whatever the explanation," he cautioned, "the possibility of long-distance sexual problems must be made clear." And he added: "We have no way of knowing if there are vasectomized men out there who are soldiering on in silence or put their trouble down to age."

The good news in Ben's case: After four months on oral testosterone, Ben was back to 100 percent erections with complete staying power. If you are having impotence problems and had a vasectomy 10 years or more ago, get your testosterone level checked. (See page 88-91 for more information on testosterone therapy.)

Ref: Royal College of General Practitioners Members' Reference Handbook, 1994.

A Few Nutrients for Impotence

If you find impotence is a major problem, I recommend that you get plenty of the following nutrients:

Vitamin E: Since vitamin E has proven abilities to help increase circulation and impotence is often caused by reduced blood flow, increasing your intake of vitamin E may help. You should be taking 400 lUs of vitamin E daily.

Eat your fish: Like vitamin E, fish oil can increase blood flow and thus help in impotence cases where decreased blood flow is the problem. Because EPA, a nutrient in fish oil, makes blood less likely to clump, it allows -blood to flow more freely, even through small capillaries.

Zinc: Zinc is essential to the proper functioning of the male reproductive system. A recent study indicated that zinc supplementation could indeed raise sperms count, increase testosterone, and give the libido a much needed spark. Take 25-50 mg daily.

Ginseng may do the trick: Animal studies have shown that stress-related sexual decline can be helped by ginseng. In Europe, where ginseng is more widely studied than in America, scientists have found that the root can improve testosterone production and give an overall feeling of well-being. Take the standard capsules found at the health food store, four to six per day.

If you think you are facing impotence, consider the poor male bee and cheer up. The lucky male, who battles thousands of competitors and finally makes it with the queen, mounts her in flight. It sounds romantic, but it's hardly that. After he finishes &*few seconds* of copulation, he peals away and his penis snaps off inside the queen, acting as a plug to prevent loss of sperm. He has had his big romance; he crashes to earth and dies.

The only mammal that has such a malignant sex life is the mouse-like marsupial called a swamp antechinus. During the brief mating season, this frantic little satyr engages in continuous copulation until he drops dead.

For Men Only —
Surgery Delivers Heaven on Earth?

Since the beginning of recorded history, man has had an inferiority complex about his penis — it isn't long enough, it isn't thick enough, or both. This is somewhat analogous to women's opinions of their own breasts — they're either too big or too small.

Except in a few cases, most women don't care that much about the size of her partner's organ. Not that women are particularly eager to participate in surveys on the subject; most of them just don't want to talk about it. Based on *very limited* data, I have concluded that *thickness* may be important to women whereas length is not. A good purchase and a sense of fullness are erotically stimulating. A very long penis looks more like a threat than an object of sexual love. A woman can visualize that thing puncturing her liver or some other non-erotic zone. That's not conducive to good lovemaking.

For some reason men fret about their organ size. That's why you can pick up many low-grade magazines that appeal to the gullible and find ads for instruments, salves, or tonics that will lengthen the phallus - none of them work and some of them may be dangerous. One crook with a sense of humor advertised that for $19.95, he would send an instrument that would give instant enlargement to the penis. He would send the pathetic pea-brain a magnifying glass by return mail.

And now surgeons have entered the penis-stretching market and promise the under-endowed heaven on earth. But, as usual in new and spectacular surgical procedures, the results often don't rise to the claims.

The lengthening operation is accomplished by freeing up the base of the penis, which is below the pubic bone, causing it to "drop forward" from its anchorage. The patient will expect a nice augmentation of two or three inches, thus qualifying him for barroom bets on a Saturday night. But according to British surgeons, he will be lucky to gain an inch and, in fact, may *lose* an inch. Why one would lose length from the surgery is not easy to explain, but I suspect it is from internal scarring that pulls the penis back to where it came from.

The thickening procedure is another matter. For a man with an unusually thin penis, the thickening operation can be a great confidence-builder and definitely make him a better sex partner. In the first thickening operations, the thickening was accomplished by extracting fat by liposuction and injecting it under the skin of the penis. The patient would be thrilled to awaken from surgery and see a pile-driver rather than a pencil. His pleasure would be short-lived as within six months or a year the fat would be reabsorbed, and he would be back with what God endowed him.

That problem has apparently been solved by the use of strips of tissue taken from the buttocks. These strips are inserted on both sides of the organ and, although there is some reabsorption, there is a definite — and apparently permanent — thickening of about 10 percent, *in most cases.* But this enhancement can also be a total failure as the tissue may be gradually absorbed. The penis may end up looking rather lopsided in some cases, but most men are willing to pay that price as long as they get that macho look of a massive organ.

If impotence is a problem, the best thing that has happened to these frustrated and depressed men is the penile prosthesis. Two plastic rods are inserted from the bottom under the scrotum all the way up to the tip on the penis. The only scar is between the legs under the scrotum and is not seen by anyone, including the patient, without a mirror.

This operation works almost every time and is highly recommended for men suffering from erection failure or failure to maintain the erection. I have sent many men to the inventor of the procedure, Dr. Michael Small in Miami, Florida, and I have never had a dissatisfied patient. With most patients, it added 20 years or more to their sex life. Many a romance and many a marriage would never have happened if it had not been for this remarkably simple surgical procedure.

I suggest that you seriously consider leaving things as they are. The thickening operation can be recommended if tissue strips are used and the surgeon is experienced in the procedure. Your costs are going to be $5,000 to $10,000. The lengthening operation is a long shot, if you will pardon the expression, and I would stay away from it.

If you have an erection problem, the penile prosthesis is the answer for 95 percent of those affected.

The Cowboy Syndrome (Have Gun Will Travail)

An Italian specialist in male hormones has reported that cowboy playboys, who try to plow through the entire female population of their city, run a high risk of early impotence — sexual burnout by age 40. His research was based on a study of 1,500 cases of impotence studied over a period of eight years. However, most men who had "regular" sex, but not marathon sex, would not face impotence until the age of 70 or beyond. So don't take the use-it-or-lose-it principle too far.

Now Just Relax

Tension is the number one killer of sexual desire. How can you perform sexually when your mind is filled with thoughts of work, bills, problems, the kids? To enjoy sex you must be there — physically and mentally. If it takes meditation, a warm bath, a quick nap, whatever, you must find a way to relax yourself so you can enjoy sex and life.

Chapter 5

A Few Tricks of the Trade for Men (and Women)

On an almost daily basis, book after book appears devoted to improving male sexual technique. I don't like these so-called guides, mostly because I find them to be sexist. Why is the onus of performance only and always on the man? If anything, it's a two-way street; it's the act of making love. Now I'm not calling for more books designed to help *women* with technique; rather I'd like to see an end to the perseveration of books and articles on sexual performance.

Both men and women should spend more time caring for their partners and caring for themselves as opposed to worrying about technique. Making love is not an athletic event; it's not something you have to practice for perfection, like tennis; it's certainly not competitive. You know the basics; the rest of it should develop naturally.

I'll go on record right now as saying, unequivocally, that what America needs is more fun in the bedroom and less worry about technique.

But with that said, there are indeed a few simple "tricks" men can use to improve their sexual function and make the act of making love fulfilling once again.

One of the simplest approaches to reviving the romantic past — and one that most women, and many men, will not approve of — is to sleep separately. Some of the experts feel that familiarity breeds contravallation and that if couples slept separately, even in different bedrooms, it might help their sex life.

The Japanese must feel that way. They are very careful about whom they will sleep with and, in fact, they will only sleep with themselves. If a Japanese couple is offered a hotel room with only one bed, they will refuse it. If they are forced to take it, one of them will sleep on the floor (I don't know which one).

Partners, at least in the U.S., think they sleep better when they share the bed. Women, I think, are more likely to adhere to this concept — it's the snuggling instinct; women like to snuggle.

Researchers at Leicestershire University in England, using electronic devices to measure movements, confirmed that people whose partners were away, or their pet was not in the bed, slept longer and more peacefully. But when researchers asked couples how they slept when alone, fewer than half thought they slept better. Without good sleep there is no good sex.

Tips to Avoid Premature Ejaculation

The bane of many men, premature orgasm is also constant fodder for female comediennes. If you persistently cannot control the timing of ejaculation, there are a few easy steps to take in order not to have your partner call you a selfish pig.

1. Slow down! Not the way you are making love, but the way you live your life. We rush to work, rush through our jobs, fight traffic, rush home, inhale dinner, and then rush through lovemaking. The faster, more stressful your life, the greater the chance of encountering premature ejaculation. Relax — spend an entire day relaxed; with a minimum of stress. Chances are your lovemaking that day will be relaxed and enjoyable, with no premature orgasm.

2. Try some exercise. I've spoken about the Kegel exercises; exercises traditionally used by pregnant women to strengthen the pelvic floor. This exercise also works for men — helping to strengthen erections and giving control over ejaculation. The instructions for the Kegel are worth repeating:

To do the Kegel you first have to identify the correct muscles. The muscles you want to strengthen are those you use to stop the flow of urine. In fact, the Kegel feels exactly the same. Find those muscles, then contract them and hold for three to five seconds. Relax for five seconds, then contract again. Start with 10 contractions, three times a day. And eventually work your way up to 50 contractions, three times a day.

Once these muscles are strengthened, it will take a month or so, use them to stop ejaculation. Squeeze just as you start to feel the urge to ejaculate, and stop all motion.

Try Some Good Old-Fashioned Exercise

Readers of my newsletters know that I am not big on exercise, particularly the Jane Fonda, run yourself into the ground, method of exercise. But for good health, lower blood pressure, and a better sex life, moderate exercise can work wonders.

Of course, exercise can help you look better (trimmer, leaner) and give you more energy. Both outcomes are sexually enhancing. But the more you exercise, the better shape you're in, the better your sex life will be. You'll be able to have sex longer, and that sex can, when you desire, be more intense.

It has been proven, as proven as medical reports can be, that men who exercise not only have better sex, but have sex more often.

Maybe it's psychological; maybe the better you feel about yourself, the more you feel like having sex. Whatever the cause, don't look a gift horse in the mouth. Exercise. I heartily recommend a 30-minute brisk walk at least three times a week. Give it a month, and I think you'll see that I am right about your sexual fitness.

One other interesting idea: Maybe you remember a report broadcast on CNN last year that indicated weight lifting is a great exercise for men and women in their 60s and 70s. Normally, we think of weight lifting as exercise for energetic, but not-too-bright, young men and women.

But the report indicated that lifting light weights increased bone mass and greatly increased strength in older Americans. Weight lifting may also have another benefit for men — better sex.

It appears that lifting weights somehow tricks your body into thinking it is growing. Maybe as muscles grow from lifting, the body interprets this as a growth spurt — much like the growth periods we have as children. At any rate, in men this growth spurt is accompanied by increased levels of testosterone. So it makes sense that lifting weights can help to charge your sex drive. I'm talking about light weights that you can easily lift 20 to 30 times per set. Leave the heavy lifting to your kids.

Try Something New

Everyone needs a little variety in their life. But all too often, while we strive to add variety in our meals, the books we read, our vacation spots, etc., we forget our sex life.

One reason is that men and women feel guilty talking about sex — even men and women who have been married for 20, 30, or 40 years. Sex is a topic about which most couples don't talk comfortably.

The result is a sexual pattern: We make love the same way time after time. Then, we're surprised when the joy and thrill of sex begin to decrease. I love a thick steak for dinner, but I wouldn't want it every night for a month.

You get the picture. Maybe it's time to try something new. But I can hear you saying, "I don't think my wife (or husband) will go for it." Maybe you're underestimating your mate. Like you, he/she may very well want some variety.

Second, I find that most people (but men, in particular), when they do decide to add new twists to lovemaking, move ahead far too quickly. The result is almost always a negative response from your partner.

Take some simple advice and go slowly when introducing a new technique. Give you and your partner a chance to see how it feels. After the first or second time, when you are both relaxed, you may find that what was not enjoyable at first is now very enjoyable.

Never give up after the first or second attempt. Try something at least three times before deciding it is not right for you or your spouse.

Sex in the Middle of the Night

Sex before sleep is as traditional as apple pie ... well, you see what I'm getting at. Who ever said that sex before sleep was the preferred method of lovemaking? I argue that before bedtime may be the worst possible time to have sex.

By the end of the day you and your partner are tired. Is this the time to make love? When you're exhausted?

Many older couples have found that an ideal time to make love is in the middle of the night. Why? Because you are calm and rested. After a few hours sleep, your energy levels rise and you're physically better prepared to make love.

Give it a try. In fact, some therapists have suggested setting an alarm for, say, 1:00 a.m.

Few know that a man's hormonal cycle peaks at dawn. So early morning sex is also a practical alternative to sex after the 11 o'clock news.

Go Easy on the Fried Foods

Forget worrying about cholesterol! But foods fried in heavy polyunsaturated (fake) fat have been shown to lower testosterone levels. So, eat your steak, but stay away from those McDonald's fries! A recent study indicated that after a meal heavy in artificial fat, a man's testosterone level could drop by as much as 30 percent.

What Do Men and Women Want?

A sense of joy and fun while making love. Remember, lovemaking is not an athletic event. Don't worry about performance or orgasms. *Have some fun!!!!* Once fun leaves the bedroom, sex is not very far behind. Enjoy yourself and your partner!

Forget Foreplay

Well, not all the time, but every once in a while, both men and women enjoy quick intercourse. No foreplay, just penetration. Studies show that prolonged foreplay often *reduces* a special type of female orgasm. That is, a rapid, strong orgasm, much like that experienced by a man.

So while foreplay is wonderful, there are times when intercourse itself should be the only item on the menu. Sound animalistic, primitive, and insensitive? (Yep.)

Deeper Penetration

Size doesn't count. Why? Because most women experience clitoral orgasm, which is the external stimulation of the clitoris, and it has nothing to do with penis size. After the first three inches, it's all bragging rights and good for nothing but barroom bets; it has nothing to do with sexual love.

But if you and your partner want deeper penetration, regardless of penis size, try the woman on top position. This position allows for the deepest penetration.

Making Love Can Be an All Day Affair

And affair is the precise word. To heighten the sexual arousal, take all day. Start with light kisses, even talk about the experience. Then let the sexual tension build over the day — at its own pace. As the day progresses, so will the anticipation. Then when you are both ready, and only then, let the experience happen. You may be surprised at how much passion a day of soft attention can generate.

The Condom

One of the nice things about getting older is that you and your partner need not worry about pregnancy. There's no need for condoms, jellies, etc. But for many men, a condom can be used to heighten sexual enjoyment. For one thing, a condom can reduce the urge to ejaculate by just enough to give you control of premature ejaculation, although this is seldom a problem for men over 50.

And for those couples who still must use condoms, here's a trick: Place a small amount of water-based lubricant on the tip of the penis before putting on the condom. This has been shown to increase feeling by making the condom more slippery.

For Fathers to Be

Men with low sperm counts can increase fertility by making love a second time one hour after the first encounter. This second ejaculation has been shown to have an increased sperm count in most men. But this holds true only for men with low sperm counts. If your sperm count is in the normal range, the second ejaculation will not contain as much sperm.

Special note: If your sperm count is low you may be exercising too much! Excessive exercise has been shown to lower male hormone levels, which, in turn, can inhibit the production of sperm.

Chapter 6

Men's Health:
The Prostate and Beyond

You know the old saying about death and taxes — the two things in this life we can be sure of. But for American men over the age of 50, I must, unfortunately, add another certainty: prostate problems.

Now don't get me wrong. It's not my intention to alarm you; and, unlike the National Cancer Institute, I'm not predicting that one-third or two-thirds of American men will eventually be diagnosed with prostate cancer. I find such statistics misleading as well as self-serving: If so many men will get prostate cancer, don't we need to allocate more money to the National Cancer Institute?

My caveat about prostate disease is meant only to make you aware of the potential problems all men face. For most men, the inconvenience will be minor — an increased need to urinate or an increased *urge* to urinate with little passage of urine. For others, the problem may involve a decline in sexual performance. I'm not making light of this situation, but it certainly isn't cancer.

Unfortunately for some, prostate problems can lead to cancer. But even in these cases, the cancer is not as serious as it sounds. Most men with prostate cancer are older — most, in fact, in their late 70s or early 80s. Prostate cancer is usually slow-moving, although not in all cases, so that most men die of natural causes well before the prostate cancer becomes a medical problem.

So you see, the recent scare tactics by the AMA and its members are yet another money-making scheme. Can you imagine an 80-year-old man undergoing prostate surgery to remove a tumor so small as to be insignificant? I can't; but a lot of doctors sure can.

But if you are experiencing some of the symptoms of an enlarged prostate (what doctors call benign prostatic hypertrophy or BPH), you are most likely suffering from worry that cancer is imminent or that sex is a thing of the past.

Calm down. *The most recent studies indicate that the best treatment for BPH is no treatment at all.* This startling conclusion was published in the *Journal of the American Medical Association,* after studies showed that most symptoms of BPH go *away by themselves*

No surgery, no drugs, no nothing. Just wait, and the chances are very good that your symptoms will disappear just as quickly as they came. Of course, the AMA suggests yearly checkups for men over 50. These may not be necessary if you are symptom-free.

I understand the psychological and physical problems related to BPH; and I know that no matter what I say, some of you will ultimately decide to have surgery, in hopes of relieving prostate problems. *Surgery is the last resort.* Do not let your doctor push you to a surgical solution. In most cases it is not necessary, and can create its own set of serious, long-term problems.

Prostate surgery is uncertain. There's the risk of infection from the surgery. Nosocomial infections (that is, infections from the hospital) are dangerous and often deadly. The extended period of healing, the cost of surgery, and the possibility of complications mean that this surgery is not to be undertaken lightly.

And of primary concern is the risk of reduced sexual function.

Some doctors will tell you that BPH surgery doesn't affect sexual function; that's simply not true. A *conservative* estimate is that sexual function is adversely affected in at least 30 percent of cases. I argue that the figure is near 60 percent.

Sure, they'll tell you that after a few months your ability to have sex will return, but that's a ruse. I've seen the few months turn into a year, then two, then ... forget it. I've always believed in the old adage, "Use it or lose it. For a man in his late 50s or early 60s, a year without sex could lead to a lifetime without sex.

I keep reading that "in time, most men will be able to enjoy sex again." That's what the urologists will tell you. They just never mention that the "time" may be extended well beyond the normal recovery time for the surgery. It's made to sound like a sure thing, but it's not. Are you willing to risk your sex life by undergoing surgery for BPH? That's the first question I'd answer before considering surgery.

The first and most serious potential problem is the inability to maintain an erection. The prostate is in a delicate area of the male anatomy — a place where muscle tissue and blood vessels feeding the penis are abundant. If during surgery muscle is damaged, there's a very good chance of impotence. Can the damage be reversed?

Maybe yes, maybe no. And how long it will take to strengthen the damaged muscles is anyone's guess. The erectile tissue in the penis is even more important than the associated muscles and they too depend on an adequate blood supply. Adequate nerve function is also vital to erection. So there are three vital tissues involved here (nerve, muscle, and erectile tissue); damage any one of these and it's all over.

For younger men, prostate surgery can make you sterile. I won't go into the physiology, but the bottom line is that semen is no longer ejaculated through the penis; it is ejaculated *backward* into the bladder — no semen, no ability to impregnate. Finally, men who have had prostate surgery can lose their ability to reach sexual climax. Again, doctors will tell you this ability will return in time. Whose time? When?

My suggestion, for anything short of prostate cancer, and even then, only in the proper cases, *do not have prostate surgery.* The risks are too great and problems created by the surgery can be *permanent.*

Taking Care of Your Prostate

Two specific changes you can make to improve the condition of your prostate and alleviate symptoms of BPH are reducing your use of prescription medications and using a few specific vitamins, minerals, and herbs.

We discuss the problem of prescription medications in chapter 4 and we've devoted an entire book to *Prostate Problems: Safe, Simple, Effective Relief.* In the meantime, here are a few common-sense steps to take:

1. Lose weight if you are truly obese: Obesity creates problems of all kinds, particularly prostate problems.

2. Cut down on your alcohol consumption: Too much alcohol adversely affects a man's sexual perform-ance, and alcohol can irritate the prostate. The prostate can contain concentrations of alcohol more than 10 times greater than in the bloodstream. All things in modera-tion, the Romans said (although they didn't follow their own advice).

3. Moderate exercise: Walking gives you energy, ex-ercises the prostate, helps you lose weight, and can im-prove your sexual energy and performance.

Natural Supplements and Your Prostate

If you haven't yet heard, the new hero of the herbal medicine club is the saw palmetto. This amazing berry has shown an amazing ability to eliminate the symptoms of BPH and reduce the size of an enlarged prostate. In fact, the *British Journal of Pharmacology* reports that the saw palmetto berry works as well or better than the drug Proscar for reducing an enlarged prostate.

But you won't read much about saw palmetto, be-cause the PDA has ruled it illegal to advertise the herb as a solution to any prostate problems. But take it from me, in many cases, saw palmetto is all you need. For an en-larged prostate, I suggest two to three capsules of saw palmetto, two to three times a day. This regimen often works, but it takes time — up to six months. To me, six months of taking saw palmetto beats unproven surgery laden with side effects.

Once the symptoms of BPH are gone, try one or two capsules once a day to keep your prostate healthy.

Add zinc to your diet. Numerous studies have clearly shown that low levels of zinc in your system will adversely affect the condition of your prostate. In fact, the prostate normally contains a higher concentration of zinc than any other organ in the body. And if you are on one of those low red meat, low calorie diets, the chances are good that you're low in zinc. The best source of the mineral is red meat.

If you are taking an iron supplement, absorption of zinc is compromised as well. Eat your meat and take 25 mg to 50 mg of zinc each day.

Take a magnesium supplement. Along with protecting your heart, magnesium has been shown to protect the urinary system and prevent the formation of stones. How magnesium works is not really known, but it can protect your heart and it may protect your prostate. Take 250 mg to 500 mg each day.

Selenium is another element that can help improve sexuality and the condition of your prostate. Selenium helps to regulate the level of male hormones and thus plays a role in maintaining a healthy prostate and a vigorous sex life. I suggest 100-200 mcg daily.

Another herb that helps to relieve the symptoms of BPH is the juniper berry. The herb is a powerful diuretic and there's some evidence it can help the prostate. The herb is available at most health food stores. One caution: take only the amount recommended by the manufacturer. Too much juniper can irritate the urinary tract.

Pumpkin seed oil has shown promise in improving the condition of the prostate. Some claim that prostate problems can be worsened by the presence of parasitic worms in the lower intestine. Pumpkin seed oil kills these worms.

Linus Pauling, who was treated for prostate cancer, recommended vitamin C for an enlarged prostate. He could be right, I don't know, but taking 500 mg of C each day is a good health policy for many reasons.

I've read some preliminary reports that show bee pollen works well to improve the condition of the prostate and increase sexual energy. Some claim bee pollen can reduce an enlarged prostate. If you are allergic to bee stings *do not* use bee pollen. There have been reports of dangerous allergic reactions in some people using this product.

Finally, some in the natural health field are recommending vitamin F to reduce BPH and eliminate the need for surgery. "Vitamin F," linoleic, and linolenic acids, have been used for prostate problems and as a preventive against kidney damage. But the case for these fatty acids is not conclusive.

The Pain and Pathos of Peyronie's

The title of this chapter is "The Prostate and Beyond." Part of the "beyond" has to do with a terrible affliction of the penis called Peyronie's Disease. It has become rather common and, like so many other things in medicine, we have no idea why some men get this awful condition and others don't.

In Peyronie's disease, there is a plaque-formation, a gristle-like growth alongside the penis that causes an abnormal bending of the organ inconsistent with intercourse. It's like trying to insert a boomerang into a milk bottle. It may be painful physically as well as mentally — a thoroughly depressing situation for a sexually active male and his partner.

Many techniques have been tried, from excising the plaque to DMSO and penile prostheses. None of these measures have proven satisfactory. The only reasonably successful method of treatment is called a Nesbit procedure. The terminology of the surgical technique is too technical for a description here, but ask your urologist for a referral to a surgeon experienced with the method.

One of our subscribers to my newsletters recently wrote in giving the following advice: "My husband suffered from a terrible disease called Peyronie's disease for several years. Then he started taking vitamin E and over a period of months, the condition resolved. He still takes vitamin E." — *Z.M.J., R.N., Washington.* I don't know if the treatment will work for everyone, but it's definitely worth a try.

An Underground Disease?

I have had a few patients over the years who have had a radically different complaint and one that may be more common than is generally realized. Their problem wasn't difficulty in delivering sex but in enjoying it. Even though they had the complete process (erection and ejaculation), they never had a normal orgasm. How can one ejaculate and not have an orgasm? It happens.

Here is a typical and sad case:

"I have a problem that may not be known to you in your practice, but I am hoping that you may have a solution. For 20 years, I have not been able to achieve any sort of sexual satisfaction. I can achieve the necessary components of sex (erection and ejaculation), but there is no pleasurable sensation from it. I came close to suicide but, over 20 years, I have come to terms with it. After many medical exams, I was sent to a psychiatrist and, after interminable talks about my mother and beating up pillows, I finally gave up and concluded that, by and large, psychological counseling is an expensive fraud. I was told about a doctor who attaches electrodes to the organ and then measures brain wave responses — sounds like more *of* the same.

"Can you offer any hope in what I assume is a rare condition?"

I had another patient in his 20s who complained to me that "an orgasm was no better than a good sneeze." The fact that the first patient had heard of a doctor who does the bizarre testing procedure described indicates that there are others out there with the same condition. I am wondering if this might be one of those "underground illnesses" that no one wants to talk about.

I have no immediate answer to this problem and I haven't any idea why it happens. Because the sex therapists have no answer, they resort to psychological hocus-pocus such as pillow-bashing and screaming. If you have this condition, you might want to try color therapy. (See my report, *Color Me Healthy.* It may sound like more witchcraft, but it is simple, inexpensive, and totally safe. What have you got to lose?

Chapter 7

Enhancing Female Sexual Response — Naturally

I hate to use the term aphrodisiac; it conjures up so many ugly myths and dangerous potions. But the fact is, there are several natural, herbal substances and a few specific exercises that can help to increase a woman's sexual response.

I'm not talking about an uncontrollable increase in sexual response, but a demonstrably improved feeling in some women.

Let's start with the basics: For both men and women, how you feel about yourself makes a tremendous difference in how well you respond to sex. If you're confident, sex is fulfilling and a creative expression of your psychological and physiological state. So before any sexually enhancing exercises or herbs can work, men and women need to take a close look at their levels of self-esteem.

If you are not happy about your physical appearance, chances are you will be reticent to explore the full range of physical, sexual possibilities. One very important note, however: Don't let culture's view of the ideal man or woman affect how you feel about yourself. In America, the ideal woman is 18, thin as a rail, and has the intelligence of a 12-year-old.

If you are in your 40s, it's simply impossible to meet this idiotic ideal. The key is to feel realistically confident about your looks. Perhaps dropping a few pounds may be necessary, but the goal isn't to be the next Twiggy. Perhaps some exercise is necessary, but the goal isn't to pass out with Jane Fonda.

Once your self-image meets your expectations, women can begin with a few exercises to improve specific muscles that come into play during sex.

From the Orient comes a cross-legged exercise that can help. Sit on a cushion or blanket on the floor in a cross-legged position. Try to get your knees close to the floor and keep your back very straight. Take a few very deep, very slow breaths to calm yourself and to get into the rhythm of the exercise. Now, as you inhale, try to draw your abdomen back toward your spine; when you exhale, slightly exaggerate the process and let your abdomen expand.

This exercise can help to stimulate the pelvic region.

From this same position, you can help to strengthen the pubococcygeus muscle. This muscle loses tone as you age and, as it does, many women experience a lessened sensitivity in the vagina. Another result is often incontinence.

To strengthen this important muscle, try tightening the vagina and the anus — drawing them both in as you inhale. Try this exercise daily — working up to a total of 20 minutes. Many women report heightened sexual response in a matter of weeks.

Now, let's take a look at some herbal ways to increase sexual response.

One fine herb to help balance female hormones and increase sexual response is called Vitex. It has been used for decades as perhaps the best herb to balance female hormones. If you can't find Vitex at your local health food store, try looking for chaste berries — this is the older name for the herb. Vitex stimulates the pituitary gland. In a woman with decreased sexual interest, Vitex can raise the sex drive. Conversely, in a women with excess sexual drive, Vitex can help bring the urge under control.

But Vitex isn't an overnight cure. It takes two to three months to stabilize and balance female hormones.

Vitex is available in pills, or can be taken as a tea.

For an almost immediate improvement in sexual response, women can try damiana. Tradition has it that a cup of damiana tea can improve the feeling during intercourse.

There's much truth to this. When damiana is excreted through the urinary tract, the herb causes a slight irritation and stimulates the genital/urinary tract. And the herb also produces a compound called nervine that has been shown to produce a mild euphoria.

Damiana can be taken as a tea, one to two hours before intercourse. The herb is bitter and will need sweetening, preferably with honey.

Some Other Herbal Aids for Women

If you are still menstruating, there's the possibility that you are experiencing some symptoms of premenstrual syndrome. If so, you fully understand that lovemaking is often the farthest thing from your mind when PMS strikes.

There are several natural methods to help alleviate and eliminate the symptoms. I've treated PMS in my practice for more than a decade, and I know these natural methods can work. But be advised — natural cures aren't overnight sensations. It takes time to balance hormonal levels; natural remedies work slowly. Give these suggestions a few months to work. Be patient. I can guarantee — almost — that you'll be pleased with the results.

Prior to menstruation, take evening primrose oil twice a day. A 500 mg tablet at breakfast and bedtime can greatly reduce the symptoms. But once menstruation begins, stop taking the capsules. Evening primrose oil can increase bleeding.

On the herbal front, I recommend dandelion tea as a great way to reduce water retention. This herb is an excellent diuretic.

I am not fond of Chinese herbs. Increasingly, the herbs sold in this country from China contain dangerous adulterants. Some have been shown to cause cancer. But Dong quai is one herb that I think is wonderful for women. During PMS, hormones are out of balance. Dong quai can rapidly reestablish the proper hormonal balance and relieve many PMS problems. *Remember*, like evening primrose oil, Dong quai should be taken prior to menstruation. Stop taking the herb once menstruation begins because it can cause excess bleeding.

Stay away from alcohol if your symptoms include depression. Alcohol won't improve your state of mind, and may worsen your depression.

Also, stay away from caffeine and sugar. Caffeine only adds to the tension and anxiety. And numerous studies show that caffeine increases breast tenderness and pain. Unrefined sugar can cause you to have large mood swings, going from the sugar rush to a sudden drop in energy. Stick to complex carbohydrates, like those found in pasta.

Try some B_6. The most popular vitamin for treating PMS is B_6. The vitamin may very well control the mood swings and give you an energy boost.

And for menstrual cramps, ginger tea offers almost immediate results (as it does for motion sickness). Boil some root for a few minutes and add honey. That's all there is to it.

Urinary Tract Infections

It's impossible for a woman to enjoy sex when she is suffering from a urinary tract infection. Most women know that at the first sign of infection it's good to increase the amount of fluid intake to help flush the system. And most women know the value of cranberry juice.

What you may not know is that 500 mg of vitamin C can be very helpful in killing the infection. The acidity of the vitamin limits bacterial growth in the bladder and urinary tract.

Another way to fight the infection is with echinacea and/or goldenseal tea. Both of these herbs are proven to fight infection quickly. Echinacea is particularly useful in all types of infections, from urinary tract to throat to ear. (As a note, if you have young children, echinacea tea tastes great and can help eliminate ear and throat infections without the need for dangerous antibiotics.)

Vaginal Yeast Infections

Another problem that can absolutely ruin sex is the vaginal yeast infection. To stop these infections before they get out of control, increase your intake of vitamins A, C, and E. Try 25,000 IU of A, at least 500 mg of C and 400 IU of E each day.

Herbal potions of goldenseal and slippery elm can help. As can the ever vigilant echinacea.

There are also steps you can take to avoid these infections.

To begin, wear only cotton underwear. Yeast infections thrive in moisture, but cotton keeps you dry. Along those same lines, wear loose clothing. Tight fitting clothes, like synthetic materials, inhibit necessary ventilation, leaving areas moist and susceptible to bacteria growth.

Stay away from public toilets (or at least take precautions). Most women worry about the cleanliness of the seat, but it's the bowl itself that is the problem. The water in the bowl is a prime means of spreading yeast infections. Make sure you flush a public toilet before you urinate. This will help eliminate any water that could be contaminated.

Finally, use a lubricant during intercourse. Natural lubricants reduce friction. Don't use petroleum jelly, nor any of the scented chemicals brands. A water-soluble lubricant is best.

One final, important thought about PMS and its treatment: *Never let a doctor give you tranquilizers for depression or menstrual pain. Tranquilizers are dangerous drugs that will only increase the problem. They are also the very quickest way to kill your desire and/or ability to have sex.*

Natural Ways to Beat Depression

When you are depressed, a sexual, loving relationship is almost out of the question. It's ironic; during depression you need the caring and comfort of your partner, but somehow the idea of that comfort is far from your mind.

Unfortunately for women, depression strikes you twice as often as it does men. And studies show that the periods of depression in women are growing in length and frequency.

Now, all people get depressed from time to time. In fact, some psychologists say that periodic depression is good, offering us a cathartic experience. But what do they know?

Depression is serious and in my book it is never welcomed. For many women, it's difficult to get out of bed when depression hits. And all too often, a visit to the doctor yields a prescription drug that does nothing for the depression, but certainly affects your health and annihilates your sex life.

Before you visit your doctor, remember that depression is natural, provided it hasn't lasted for weeks, or has caused you to remain almost chained to the bed.

There are some proven, natural methods you can use to fight minor depression. These should be tried first, before other, more serious treatments are employed.

Increase your intake of B complex vitamins: The full range of B vitamins has been shown to have a calming effect on the nerves. They can help take the edge of the anxiety and nervousness that often lead to depression, so take them at the first sign.

A note for women on the pill: If you are taking birth-control pills, you are more likely to face depression than other women, and you almost always have low levels of B-complex vitamins. I believe the two are linked.

Vitamin B_{12} is particularly important. When depressed, your energy levels drop; consequently you feel lifeless and this only increases the depression. Vitamin B_{12} helps by giving you a boost of energy and a general feeling of well-being. Both are critical in beating depression.

Increase your intake of calcium and magnesium. Low levels of both calcium and magnesium have been linked to depression. In older women, low estrogen levels create low levels of calcium, which in turn depletes calcium in the system and may contribute to depression. This may be the reason why postmenopausal women are more prone to depression.

Magnesium is also important to overall mental and physical well-being. Studies have shown that depressed patients usually have low levels of magnesium.

Tyrosine: L-tyrosine is an amino acid which plays a major role in the body's production of norepinephrine. You may know that norepinephrine is a chemical your body makes to make you feel better, calmer, happier, enthusiastic. Take 50 mg, twice daily.

Watch your diet: There's a chance your depression could be triggered by what you eat, similar to an allergic reaction. The usual culprits are refined sugars.

Exercise: It may be the last thing on your mind, but exercise, even a quick walk around the block, can do wonders for your state of mind. As you concentrate on breathing, moving, and coordinating your movements, you're freeing your mind from depression. It doesn't take a Zen master to see that exercise can work like meditation to free you from depression.

Finally, if you can't exercise do something, anything. When you're depressed, the worst thing to do is to sit wallowing in your depression. Do something! Rake the yard, wash the car, mow the lawn, clean the kitchen, do anything that gets you moving and keeps your mind from becoming fixed on the depression.

Menopause and Sex

Many women have told me (as their doctor, of course) that their sex lives were the most fulfilling during their 40s. There was no longer the pressure of youth, and women were so fully aware of their bodies and their emotional needs that they were able to adapt their sexuality to meet these demands.

Study after study has shown that as long as women in their 40s have a partner who is willing to experiment with sex until the right combination of frequency and intensity is found, sexuality during this time is as close to ideal as possible.

Only one cloud remains, however, for women: the worry about menopause and what this naturally occurring phenomenon will do to their bodies and their sexuality.

When sexual changes occur during the decade of the 40s and 50s, they will happen in response to the body's decline in estrogen production. This decline normally takes place between the ages of 45 and 50. The median age for the completion of menopause is approximately 51.

Menopause is a natural physical reaction to aging. There's little spectacular about the process; it has been happening to women since 51 years after the creation of Eve. And over the thousands of years women have been on this earth, the median age has remained almost constant.

Here's my point: much of the difficulty women and men have with menopause is caused by the media, including pop psychologists. Believe me, 50 years ago, menopause was not seen as a problem. Women had no negative expectations about the so-called difficulties brought on by menopause.

Our grandparents had no fear of menopause or the dreaded male "mid-life crisis." And for the most part, menopause caused no problems. Today, thanks to the media, we expect women to be cold, distant, emotionally unstable, unsexy, and unwanted. And that's how some of them have responded.

Why do you think estrogen therapy — *something to be avoided in most cases* — became so popular? Women want to avoid the horrendous consequences that the media tells them menopause will bring. Having said that, you *may* need estrogen. If so, be sure that your doctor understands the difference between Premarin (made from the urine of mares) which is prescribed by 99 percent of the gynecologists, and the natural form of estrogen which is safe and non-cancer causing.

In short, the myths surrounding menopause and its effect on sexuality are more dangerous than menopause itself. A study performed by the University of Chicago showed that the discomfort and problems associated with menopause were greatly exaggerated in the minds of women *who had never experienced any of the so-called problems.* Women who have not gone through menopause are more frightened of it than are those who have been through the experience. Don't mothers and daughters communicate anymore?

Menopause does have one symptom and that's hot flashes. For some women these flashes are a real problem. But for most women, they're usually just a minor inconvenience.

Hot flashes are related to decreased estrogen — which is really what menopause is all about. They're not dangerous, and they do not indicate any underlying problem. When you experience hot flashes, measurable changes take place in heart rate and skin temperature. Blood vessels on the skin dilate, causing your skin to indeed flush.

But knowing that the flashes won't harm you should help you cope with the episodes. Hot flashes don't cause pain, and they last for such a short time (less than three minutes in most cases) that any hormone replacement therapy to calm the flashes seems scarcely worth the risk of side effects.

The loss of estrogen can create some changes in the body. Vaginal lubrication may decrease, and some women (not all) may find sexual intercourse less enjoyable because of a dry, sometimes painful feeling. But this problem is easily solved with one of the over-the-counter lubrication jellies, such as K-Y. Vaginal dryness should not affect the ability to have an orgasm — as so many women think.

The lining of the vagina may get thinner and this can cause dyspareunia, pain with cracking and/or bleeding of the mucous membranes during intercourse. If this occurs with any regularity, it may be wise to see your physician. As mentioned above, natural estrogen may be the answer.

Another result of menopause can be an increase in vaginal infections. This is due to the decreased acidity of postmenopausal secretions. Left untreated, an infection may spread to the bladder, causing cystitis. If you suffer from cystitis, drinking two pints of cranberry juice every day might help, but antibiotics are usually necessary.

Vaginal infections can also cause vaginitis, an inflammation of the vagina. To treat vaginitis, try a yogurt douche (any flavor!) twice daily. The "friendly" bacteria contained in yogurt will help fight the infection.

Other menopausal changes can involve a slight reduction in the size of the clitoris — but this in no way affects the ability to achieve orgasm or the intensity of the orgasm.

Remember, these natural changes need not affect sexuality. And in many cases, women do not experience any of these physical changes. The bottom line is this: little or nothing happens during menopause to affect or reduce your ability to have and enjoy sex. What can affect your sexuality is the fear, the unfounded fear, of menopause and the hyperbolic portrayal of post-menopausal women by the media and by psychologists eager for a trip to the "Donahue Show."

How Hormones Can Help Prevent Breast Cancer

Believe it or not, doctors have had remarkable success with testosterone therapy for postmenopausal women. I think the biggest surprise is the discovery of how absolutely vital the hormone is for females. While "anabolic therapy," as it is called, has been grossly neglected in males, it is essentially unheard of in the treatment of females. That's why this article is *must* reading for both sexes.

Although a female only needs ten percent of the testosterone level men need for maximum health, they need this ten percent just as much as men need their proper quota. Many postmenopausal women have essentially *no* testosterone. So they have *two* major problems: menopause *and* andropause. Now, that's just not fair!

Testosterone is effective in the treatment and prevention of bone loss. That means it's a natural for treating osteoporosis. For many years, estrogen has been used to treat osteoporosis, but the results have been inconclusive. I think it's a waste of time and money, to say nothing of the cancer risk. Testosterone therapy is clearly more effective than estrogen and safer (completely safe, in fact).

Many of you know that I have decried the indiscriminate use of synthetic estrogen and synthetic progesterone (the two female hormones) for years, because there is strong evidence that they are carcinogenic, especially concerning cancer of the breast. In regard to the use of synthetic testosterone, let me remind you that I have not abandoned all of conventional medicine and I have not accepted uncritically all of alternative medicine - there is some good and bad to be found in both.

It is true that there is an increase in the incidence of breast cancer in women taking synthetic estrogen (Premarin). But natural estrogen seems to be unrelated to breast cancer as there is an *increase* in this disease after menopause, when estrogen decreases. Put another way, a woman's intrinsic estrogen (and progesterone, the other female hormone) seem to be protective and the synthetics, cancer-promoting. But the testosterone factor, usually ignored in this equation, may be far more important than both of the female hormones put together.

After menopause, there is a dramatic decrease in androgens (testosterone). These androgens are protective against breast cancer and are probably the key to prevention. It has been assumed that the changes seen after menopause in women — the deepening voice, the increase in hair, an increase in libido — are due to a relative increase in testosterone.

But the opposite seems to be true. This is a little confusing, because testosterone definitely drops off at menopause; it doesn't increase. Have we been missing the boat here? We know that progesterone is protective against breast cancer. But testosterone is 1,000 times more protective than progesterone.

It seems to me that we need to stop thinking of estrogen, progesterone, and testosterone as "male" or "female" hormones, because they are probably equally important, in the right proportion, in both sexes. It's certainly true in women and so it follows, at least to me, that the same will prove to be true in men. As Dr. Wilkinson's physicist patient found out on his own, *balance* is the key.

C.W. Lovell, M.D., of the Baton Rouge Menopause Clinic, has confirmed the importance of hormonal balance in the prevention of breast cancer. In the treatment of 4,000 patients, in which he used a combination of estrogen (estradiol) and testosterone, he has reduced the incidence of breast cancer to *less than half the* national average. Using another statistic, his results are even more impressive. On average, there is one cancer discovered for every 100 mammograms performed. In those patients on testosterone therapy, there is only one cancer in every 1,000 mammograms — a decrease of 90 percent!

For more information on testosterone therapy, contact the folks at Broda O. Barnes Research Foundation (P.O. Box 98, Trumbill, CT 06611, 203-261-2101).

Testosterone therapy is just a part of what these wonderful people do. They attempt to balance the endocrine system and testosterone is just one component of that.

Conclusion

Secrets of the Heart

Well, I hope you have enjoyed this filthy little book. Even though I did considerable research for it, sex still seems tragic, comical, and a little mysterious to me. But I don't think I would have it any other way.

We have come a long way in our attitudes about sex since the time of Sir Thomas Browne, eminent physician and renowned author. He was the star witness in the Norwich witchcraft trial that resulted in the burning at the stake of Amy Duny and Rose Cullender for having intercourse with the devil.

Browne was a man of science and so clearly not prejudiced in the case as witnessed by his writings on sex: "I could be content that we might procreate like trees, without conjunction, or that there were any way to perpetuate the world without this trivial and vulgar way of coition: it is the foolishest act a wise man commits in all his life; nor is there any thing that will more deject his cool'd imagination, when he shall consider what an odd and unworthy piece of folly he hath committed."

Sex is more important to some people than to others. Many people just don't care about sex and they are glad it's over. Some of them *never* cared about sex and that includes men as well as women. They may not be any happier than the rest of us, but they have one less thing to worry about.

Most Americans have been conditioned by the media to think that everyone else is feasting at a sexual banquet to which they, the sexually deprived, were not invited. However, the following statistics from the Chicago report should make you feel remarkably normal:

• Most Americans are not interested in the kinky stuff and oral sex was third in sexual preference behind "Watching partner undress"!

• An overwhelming majority of both men and women had never cheated on their partner.

• The number of homosexuals in America is far lower than the litany we are constantly exposed to from the press and homosexual advocates — the magical statistic of ten percent. The figures are closer to 2.7 percent for men and 1.3 percent for women.

• Whether married or not, most Americans are largely monogamous. Over a lifetime, the typical male has six partners and a woman has two.

• In summary, sex in America is ruled by the three M's: Marriage, Monogamy, and the Missionary Position.

Not surprisingly, the Chicago report threw the overbearing and obnoxious publisher of the number one porn magazine in America, *Penthouse,* into a rage: "Positively, outrageously stupid and unbelievable," he snarled in his inimitable way.

Helen Gurley Brown, the editor of America's leading sex magazine for women, *Cosmopolitan* (way ahead of *Playgirl),* didn't like the report either.

The study confirmed similar reports from England and (surprise) France. The statistics for the three countries are almost identical. In all three countries, if you exclude the teens and 20s, sex is really no big deal.

Humans have a wide variation in their need for sex and you have to take that into consideration when evaluating the Chicago report. Animals have a more definite pattern within their species. Whereas the fly will copulate practically constantly, the albatross may go years between sexual encounters.

Calvin Coolidge, the president who hardly ever said anything about anything, actually said more than two words when on a visit to a poultry farm. His wife was shown a rooster that was said to have sex 400 times a day. She was very impressed and replied: "Hmm, tell that to the president when he comes round." They did, he perked up in surprise and asked: "With the same hen?"

Maybe you're an albatross or maybe you're a fly or a rooster. Either way doesn't mean that you are abnormal; everybody is different and has different sexual needs — or no needs. As Dr. Glenn Wilson, a London University psychologist remarked: "When romantic love wanes, as sooner or later it does, a marriage will stand or fall on basic compatibility and friendship."

In 1986, the National Marriage Guidance Council in England issued a report that surprised no one: "Marriage is a sexless institution for thousands of couples after only a few years of married life. Many couples are active sexually before marriage and enjoy a good married sex life in the early years of their marriage. But then, seemingly unaccountably, it tails off and suddenly there is not much sex in the marriage. It is one of the most common problems but also one that people do not like to acknowledge. They laugh about it without admitting they're suffering."

Well, I doubt that most of them are "suffering." The English press, when it comes to sex, is no different from ours.

I was at a dinner party in the countryside in England, the home of a young member of the House of Lords who had inherited the title from his father. They were a charming couple in their late 30s with two children. Halfway through dinner, the topic somehow got on to sex. The hostess said nothing for awhile, but then gave her thoughts in no uncertain terms: "You know, we worry about young people engaging in sex before marriage and then, after marriage, there is *no* sex." I was a little embarrassed and dared not look at the husband who pretended not to hear the remark. It didn't seem to me to be the place for the wife to be upbraiding her husband for not putting out.

Mark Twain, one of the greatest writers of all time, in my opinion, said : "A woman is only a woman, but a cigar is a *smoke.*" But, like most humorists, he was really just making a joculism which unsophisticated people took seriously. Here's what he *really* thought: "Love seems the swiftest, but is the slowest, of all growths. No man or woman really knows what perfect love is until they have been married a quarter of a century."

William Congreve was bitten by the love bug way back in the 16th century. He didn't call it sex, but he knew which sex to blame for his predicament:

"Ask all the tyrants of thy sex, if their fools are not known by this party-colored livery — I am melancholy when thou art absent; look like an ass when thou art present; wake for thee, when I should sleep, and even dream of thee, when I am awake; sigh much, drink little, eat less, court solitude, am grown very entertaining to myself, and (as I am informed) very troublesome to everybody else. If this be not love, it is madness, and then it is pardonable — nay yet a more certain sign than all this; I give thee my money."

The Power of the Heart

I had a good friend years ago who had been married to the same woman for 50 years. They were quite wealthy and, in fact, so rich that they could donate an entire concert hall to the city. He died of a stroke. His wife, although in perfect health and very well heeled, died six weeks later. The cause of her death was never ascertained. As far as could be determined, her heart just quit. I believe she died of a broken heart.

Scientists, including me, have always shrugged at this diagnosis as a cause of death, but the results of recent neurological research indicate that it's not just an old wives' tale; people *do* die of a broken heart. There is a part of the brain, called the insular cortex, that links the heart to thought and emotion. *Unresolvable emotional conflict* can be lethal. It's long been known that severe and unresolvable stress can flood the heart with dangerous chemicals, but what goes on in the brain to cause the catastrophe has been a complete mystery.

The new findings, as a result of work done at Johns Hopkins University, help to explain people dying from the "Voodoo curse." Dr. Stephen M. Oppenheimer, who did the research at Hopkins, said: "If you truly believe that you are going to die because someone told you so, then that becomes a tremendous, unresolvable stress."

Doctors can have the same effect as witch doctors on some suggestible people, especially in the patient who has too much faith in doctors: "You have liver cancer and six months to live." They usually die right on schedule. The victim of a broken heart is subject to the same lethal forces except, in these cases, you are your own voodoo doctor.

Interestingly, my friend had been in mediocre health for the last 20 years of his life because of severe emphysema, so there was no sex in their relationship. But the bond between them was deep. That's because sex is not love and love is not sex. Let me tell you about the love story I mentioned in an earlier chapter. It's about Nobel laureate Richard Feynman and his first and eternal love Arlene Greenbaum.

Richard met Arlene in high school and she slowly, through college, became an integral part of his life. In his junior year, he asked her to become engaged. She accepted feeling that, in time, she would be able to tame and civilize this brash, brilliant cut-up and iconoclast.

There was never a moment's uncertainty in their feelings of the permanence of their relationship. But there was considerable uncertainty in the minds of others.

Arlene developed a lump on her neck that would come and go. The doctors misdiagnosed Arlene as having cancer — Hodgkin's disease, a death sentence. Although knowing that Arlene faced certain death, he asked her to marry him. As they had made a pact long ago that their relationship was forever, she accepted.

But in 1941, things were not so simple in terms of marriage. At the time, as a graduate student, he was living off fellowships. He made the mistake of telling one of the university deans that his fiance was dying and that he wanted to marry her. He was shocked and dismayed when the professor said his fellowship would be revoked if he married her!

He did not hesitate to make immediate plans to leave graduate school for a job outside academia, but then things dramatically changed — the doctors finally realized that what they were dealing with was glandular tuberculosis. Although not treatable by any effective means — that came ten years later — it was not an immediate death sentence and there was always the possibility that the body would triumph over TB; many had done so. They could now put marriage off and continue life as it was, with Arlene concentrating on beating the White Plague with, of course, the constant attention and support of a devoted man, Richard Feynman, probably the greatest scientific genius of the 20th century.

But society, the scientific community, and family would not leave them alone. Scientific opinion at the time was adamantly opposed to marriage to a "consumptive": "Many a young consumptive mother," said Dr. Lawrence F. Flick with a rather literary turn of expression, "gets her shroud shortly after she has purchased the christening frock for her babe."

The 1937 Manual of Tuberculosis for Nurses warned that pregnancy could be fatal to the consumptive patient. There was no doubt that this was true.

His mother made the fatal mistake of opposing the marriage and alienated her beloved Richard for the rest of her life. "People dread TB," she said. "When you have a wife in a TB sanitarium, everyone knows it is not a real marriage ... you are not getting *any* of the real pleasures, but only the severe burden ... a noble but useless gesture ... a selfish thing to do, just to please one person ... I was surprised to learn such a marriage is not unlawful. It ought to be."

They went ahead with the marriage, agreeing that they would not have sex because of the twin dangers of infecting Richard and the dangers of pregnancy. A few days before driving to Arlene's Cedarhurst family home to take her for marriage, he wrote a tender note to her. It ended: "I know we both have a future ahead of us — with a world of happiness — now and forever."

He borrowed a station wagon from a friend, as he would not ask for help from his alienated family, put a mattress in the back for Arlene if needed because of the strain of the trip, and picked her up at home. She met him in a pretty white dress. They crossed New York Harbor on their honeymoon ship, the Staten Island Ferry, and were married without the presence of friends or family in a municipal office, witnessed by two strangers called in from the adjoining room.

After the brief ceremony, he kissed her on the cheek because of the real danger of infection. He helped her slowly down the stairs and then drove them to Arlene's new home — a charity hospital in New Jersey.

He moved to Los Alamos, New Mexico in 1943 to work on the atomic bomb project (it undoubtedly would have been built without him, but it would have taken longer). He put Arlene in a TB sanitarium in Albuquerque and hitchhiked to see her on weekends. He could see her slowly wasting away and knew, in his heart, that he was going to lose her. Funds were also wasting away as there was a shortfall of $300 between his meager income as a major player in the most important military-scientific project in history ($380 a month) and the expenses of the sanitarium. With the savings they had left, and the sale of the piano and a ring, they could cover just ten more months. That turned out not to be a problem.

Time was growing short and "Putzie" made a decision: They would make love and consummate a marriage that really needed no consummation. She wrote to him: "Darling, I'm beginning to think that perhaps this restlessness I feel within myself is due to pent-up emotions — I really think we'd both feel happier and better, dear, if we released our desires."

Her letter was filled with hope and determination: "I'll be all a woman would be to you — I'll always be your sweetheart and first love — I'll show you what I mean Sunday."

Her weight fell to 84 pounds and Richard began to despair. Her periods stopped, bringing the joy, and unspoken fear, of pregnancy. Unschooled in the esoterica of medicine, they did not realize that the cessation of menses was yet another sign of impending death. A pregnancy test came back negative. There must be some mistake, they thought. She began to spit up blood again and that was a message they understood. He was gripped with fear. "Keep hanging on," he urged her. There was a new drug called streptomycin that seemed to work miracles, he told her. It would be available soon.

Soon after this letter to her, he received a call from the sanitarium and was told that Arlene was dying. He borrowed the car of a colleague, Dr. Klaus Fuchs, who was later to become famous in a different way, and rushed to her bedside. He sat with her until the breathing stopped and the nurse told him she was dead. Streptomycin became available two years later, 1947, and the great scourge was brought under control.

He got up and left the sanitarium calmly. He told his colleagues the next morning not to give him any special attention. He showed little outward appearance of grief. He was ordered home on leave and, a few weeks later, received a coded telegram to return to Los Alamos immediately. He got back just in time to witness the explosion of the first atomic bomb, a project in which he had played such an important part.

A year later at Cornell, he seemed unchanged with still no sign of grief. But in the fall of that year, 1946, he broke his silence, at least to himself, and wrote a letter to Arlene. It was filled with grief, loneliness, and sorrow, his Song of Songs to the woman he worshiped. It started, "I adore you, sweetheart." and ended with: "P.S. Please excuse my not mailing this — but I don't know your new address." That's the closest he ever came to admitting to a belief in a life hereafter. Dr. Feynman could have died of a broken heart but he didn't; he had important work to do.

Some time later, he was walking along a row of shops and noticed a pretty dress in a window. A thought forced itself on him: "Arlene would like that." For the first time, he wept.

Sex is not love and love is not sex.

"My beloved is unto me as a cluster of sapphire in the vineyards of Engedi. Behold, thou art fair, my love, behold, there art fair.... My beloved speaks and says to me: 'Arise, my love, my fair one, and come away; for lo the winter is past, the rain is over and gone. The flowers appear on the earth, the time of singing has come, and the voice of the turtle dove is heard in our land....[5]" (Song of Songs)

Dr. Feynman, years later, heard the voice of the turtle dove for a second time. He was a very lucky man indeed. I've heard it, and I hope that you have too. Whenever you stop loving, and that doesn't necessarily include sexing, you might as well stop living.

The material on Richard and Arlene Feynman was derived from *Genius — Richard Feynman and Modern Physics* by James Gleick, Little, Brown — London.

Index

A

Aging, 3, 12, 1648, 22, 29-31, 33, 39, 86
Alcohol, 45, 46, 48, 71, 80 .
American Medical Association (AMA), 44, 68
Anabolic therapy, 89
Androgens, 90
Antidepressants, 44, 48
Antihistamine, 48
Antihypertensives, 44

B

Bee pollen, 73
Blood-pressure medication, 35
Bly, Robert, 18
Bonobos chimps, 6
BPH, 48, 49, 68-73
British Journal of Pharmacology, 71
Broda O. Barnes Research Foundation, 91
Brown, Helen Gurley, 94
Browne, Sir Thomas, 93

C

Calcium, 84
Chinese herbs, 80
Cholesterol, 40, 62
Clitoris, 64, 88
Coenzyme Q10, 39
Color Me Healthy, 75
Condoms, 21, 64, 65
Congreve, William, 96
Coolidge, Calvin, 95
Cortisone, 45
Cosmopolitan, 94
Courtship, 11
Cowboy Syndrome, 17, 54
Cullender, Rose, 93
Curious Customs of Sex and Marriage, 10
Cystitis, 88

D

Damiana, 79
Dandelion tea, 80
Depression, 80, 83-85
Desire, 15, 16, 33, 47, 55, 60, 83
Dong quai, 80
Drugs, 43-49, 68, 83
Duny, Amy, 93
Dyspareunia, 87

E

Echinacea, 81, 82
Economist, 6
Eicosapentaenoic acid
    (EPA), 39, 51
Ejaculation, 33, 34, 37,
    45, 58, 59, 64, 65, 74
Energy, 14, 37, 38, 48,
    60, 62, 71, 73, 81, 84
Erection, 14, 32, 33, 36,
    44, 47, 49, 54, 69, 70,
    74
Eroticism, 3, 19-21
Estrogen therapy, 86
Evening primrose oil, 80
Exercise, 20, 21, 30, 31,
    35, 36, 59, 60, 65, 71,
    78, 84, 85

F

Fatty acids, 73
Fertility, 65
Feynman, Richard, 98,
    99, 103
Fish, 39, 51
Flick, Dr. Lawrence F., 99
Food and Drug
    Administration
    (FDA), 38, 71
Foreplay, 20, 33, 63
Fuchs, Dr. Klaus, 101
Fun, 23, 27, 32, 34, 57, 63

G

Gabor, Zsa Zsa, 28
Garlic, 40, 45
Germany, 6, 7
Ginger tea, 81
Ginseng, 51
Goldenseal tea, 81
Good Health Report, 27
Greenbaum, Arlene, 98
Guilt, 24, 25

H

Hindus, 34
Hormone levels, 49, 65
Hot flashes, 87
Hypertension, 45, 48

I

Impotence, 13, 14, 33,
    44-51, 53-55, 69
Intimacy, 21, 23
Iron, 72

J

*Journal of the American
    Medical Association*,
    68
Juniper berry, 72

K

Kegel exercises, 59

L

L-carnitine, 40
L-tryptophan, 38
Lancet, 41
Lecithin, 40
Libido, 36, 38, 43, 51, 90
Love and sex, 9, 10, 12
Lovell, C.W., M.D., 90

M

Magnesium, 45, 72, 84
Marcus, Laura, 28
Masturbation, 7, 24
Meditation, 55, 85
Menopause, 14, 17, 32, 85-90
Menstrual cramps, 81
Mid-life crisis, 86
Middle-age, 16
Monogamy, 14, 94
Myths, 5, 16, 22, 28, 77, 86

N

National Cancer Institute, 67
National Marriage Guidance Council, 95
National Survey of Sexual Attitudes, 28

Nature, 35, 46
Nesbit procedure, 74
Norwich witchcraft trial, 93
Nutrients, 39, 50
Nutrition, 39, 40

O

Oppenheimer, Dr. Stephen M., 97
Options, 28
Organic farming, 41
Orgasm, 7, 20, 22, 24, 33, 34, 44, 45, 58, 59, 63, 74, 75, 87, 88

P

Pauling, Linus, 72
Penile prostheses, 74
Penthouse, 94
Performance, 17, 23, 30, 34, 45, 47, 57, 63, 67, 71
Pesticides, 41
Petty, Dr. Richard, 49
Peyronie's disease, 73, 74
Premarin, 86, 89
Premenstrual syndrome (PMS), 79, 80-82
Prescription medications, 3, 43, 70
Prostate, 3, 17, 40, 47-49, 67-73

Public toilets, 82
Pubococcygeus muscle,
    78
Pumpkin seed oil, 72

R
Ruth, Dr., 18

S
Saw palmetto, 71
Scott, George, 10
Selenium, 72
Self-love, 25
Seminal fluid, 33
Sexual response, 3, 23,
    45, 77-79
Sleeping pills, 38
Small, Dr. Michael, 54
Social Organization of
    Sexuality, 28
Stern, 7
Stress, 14, 16, 19, 36, 44,
    47, 51, 59, 97, 98
Supplements, 38, 39, 71

T
Tension, 5, 55, 64, 81
Testosterone levels, 50, 63

Testosterone therapy, 50,
    88, 89, 91
Touching, 20, 21
Tranquilizers, 44, 82, 83
Twain, Mark, 96
Tyrosine, 84

V
Vaginal yeast infection,
    82
Vitamin B$_{12}$, 84
Vitamin C, 39, 73, 81
Vitamin E, 45, 50, 51, 74
Vitex, 79

W
Weight, 35, 60, 70, 71,
    101
Weight lifting, 60
Well-Man clinic, 49
*What You Must Know
    About the Poisons in
    Your Medicine Chest*, 48
Wilkinson, Dr., 90
Wilson, Dr. Glenn, 95

Z
Zinc, 40, 51, 72

About Doctor William Campbell Douglass II

Dr. Douglass reveals medical truths, and deceptions, often at risk of being labeled heretical. He is consumed by a passion for living a long healthy life, and wants his readers to share that passion. Their health and well-being comes first. He is anti-dogmatic, and unwavering in his dedication to improve the quality of life of his readers. He has been called "the conscience of modern medicine," a "medical maverick," and has been voted "Doctor of the Year" by the National Health Federation. His medical experiences are far reaching-from battling malaria in Central America - to fighting deadly epidemics at his own health clinic in Africa - to flying with U.S. Navy crews as a flight surgeon - to working for 10 years in emergency medicine here in the States. These learning experiences, not to mention his keen storytelling ability and wit, make Dr. Douglass' newsletters (Daily Dose and Real Health) and books uniquely interesting and fun to read. He shares his no-frills, no-bull approach to health care, often amazing his readers by telling them to ignore many widely-hyped good-health practices (like staying away from red meat, avoiding coffee, and eating like a bird), and start living again by eating REAL food, taking some inexpensive supplements, and doing the pleasurable things that make life livable. Readers get all this, plus they learn how to burn fat, prevent cancer, boost libido, and so much more. And, Dr. Douglass is not afraid to challenge the latest studies that come out, and share the real story with his readers. Dr. William C. Douglass has led a colorful, rebellious, and crusading life. Not many physicians would dare put their professional reputations on the line as many times as this courageous healer has. A vocal opponent of "business-as-usual" medicine, Dr. Douglass has championed patients' rights and physician commitment to wellness throughout his career. This dedicated physician has repeatedly gone far beyond the call of duty in his work to spread the truth about alternative therapies. For a full year, he endured economic and physical hardship to work with physicians at the Pasteur Institute in St. Petersburg, Russia, where advanced research on photoluminescence was being conducted. Dr. Douglass comes from a distinguished family of physicians. He is the fourth generation Douglass to practice medicine, and his son is also a physician. Dr. Douglass graduated from the University of Rochester, the Miami School of Medicine, and the Naval School of Aviation and Space Medicine.

You want to protect those you love from the health dangers the authorities aren't telling you about, and learn the incredible cures that they've scorned and ignored?
Subscribe to the free Daily Dose updates "...the straight scoop about health, medicine, and politics." by sending an e-mail to real_sub@agoramail.net with the word "subscribe" in the subject line.

If you knew of a procedure that could save thousands, maybe millions, of people dying from AIDS, cancer, and other dreaded killers....

Would you cover it up?

It's unthinkable that what could be the best solution ever to stopping the world's killer diseases is being ignored, scorned, and rejected. But that is exactly what's happening right now.

The procedure is called "photoluminescence". It's a thoroughly tested, proven therapy that uses the healing power of the light to perform almost miraculous cures.

This remarkable treatment works its incredible cures by stimulating the body's own immune responses. That's why it cures so many ailments--and why it's been especially effective against AIDS! Yet, 50 years ago, it virtually disappeared from the halls of medicine.

Why has this incredible cure been ignored by the medical authorities of this country? You'll find the shocking answer here in the pages of this new edition of Into the Light. Now available with the blood irradiation Instrument Diagram and a complete set of instructions for building your own "Treatment Device". Also includes details on how to use this unique medical instrument.

Into the Light

Rhino Publishing S.A.
www.rhinopublish.com

Dr. Douglass' Complete Guide to Better Vision

A report about eyesight and what can be done to improve it naturally. But I've also included information about how the eye works, brief descriptions of various common eye conditions, traditional remedies to eye problems, and a few simple suggestions that may help you maintain your eyesight for years to come.
-William Campbell Douglass II, MD

The Hypertension Report.
Say Good Bye to High Blood Pressure.

An estimated 50 million Americans have high blood pressure. Often called the "silent killer" because it may not cause symptoms until the patient has suffered serious damage to the arterial system. Diet, exercise, potassium supplements chelation therapy and practically anything but drugs is the way to go and alternatives are discussed in this report.

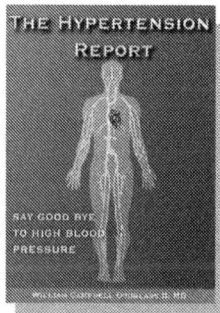

Grandma Bell's A To Z Guide To Healing With Herbs.

This book is all about - coming home. What I once believed to be old wives' tales - stories long destroyed by the new world of science - actually proved to be the best treatment for many of the common ailments you and I suffer through. So I put a few of them together in this book with the sincere hope that Grandma Bell's wisdom will help you recover your common sense, and take responsibility for your own health. -William Campbell Douglass II, MD

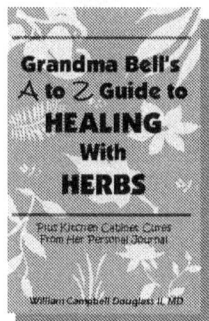

Prostate Problems:
Safe, Simple, Effective Relief for Men over 50.

Don't be frightened into surgery or drugs you may not need. First, get the facts about prostate problems... know all your options, so you can make the best decisions. This fully documented report explains the dangers of conventional treatments, and gives you alternatives that could save you more than just money!

Color me Healthy
The Healing Powers of Colors

"He's crazy!"
"He's got to be a quack!"
"Who gave this guy his medical license?"
"He's a nut case!"

In case you're wondering, those are the reactions you'll probably get if you show your doctor this report. I know the idea of healing many common ailments simply by exposing them to colored light sounds far-fetched, but when you see the evidence, you'll agree that color is truly an amazing medical breakthrough.

*When I first heard the stories,
I reacted much the same way.
But the evidence so
convinced me, that I had to
try color therapy in my practice.
My results were truly amazing.*

-William Campbell Douglass II, MD

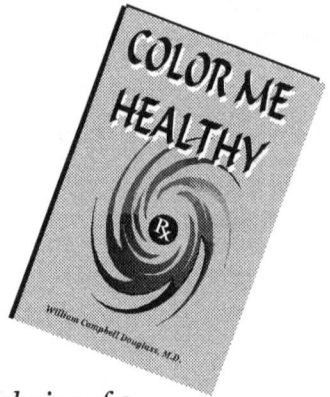

Order your complete set of Roscolene filters (choice of 3 sizes) to be used with the "Color Me Healthy" therapy. The eleven Roscolene filters are # 809, 810, 818, 826, 828, 832, 859, 861, 866, 871, and 877. The filters come with protective separator sheets between each filter. The color names and the Roscolene filter(s) used to produce that particular color, are printed on a card included with the filters and a set of instructions on how to fit them to a lamp.

What Is Going on Here?

Peroxides are supposed to be bad for you. Free radicals and all that. But now we hear that hydrogen peroxide is good for us. Hydrogen peroxide will put extra oxygen in your blood. There's no doubt about that. Hydrogen peroxide costs pennies. So if you can get oxygen into the blood cheaply and safely, maybe cancer (which doesn't like oxygen), emphysema, AIDS, and many other terrible diseases can be treated effectively. Intravenous hydrogen peroxide rapidly relieves allergic reactions, influenza symptoms, and acute viral infections.

No one expects to live forever. But we would all like to have a George Burns finish. The prospect of finishing life in a nursing home after abandoning your tricycle in the mobile home park is not appealing. Then comes the loss of control of vital functions the ultimate humiliation. Is life supposed to be from tricycle to tricycle and diaper to diaper? You come into this world crying, but do you have to leave crying? I don't believe you do. And you won't either after you see the evidence. Sounds too good to be true, doesn't it? Read on and decide for yourself.

-William Campbell Douglass II, MD

Rhino Publishing S.A.
www.rhinopublish.com

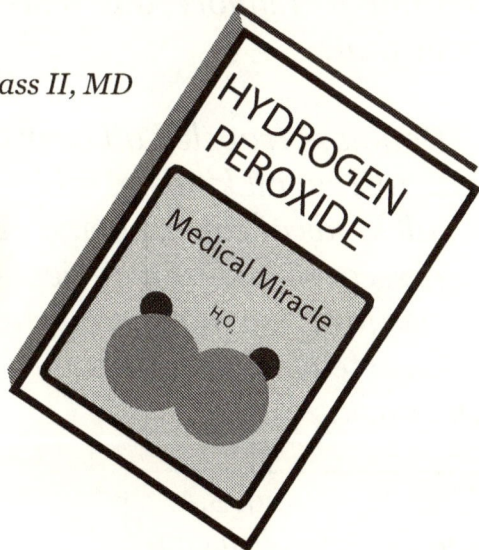

HYDROGEN PEROXIDE
Medical Miracle
H_2O_2

Don't drink your milk!

If you knew what we know about milk... BLEECHT! All that pasteurization, homogenization and processing is not only cooking all the nutrients right out of your favorite drink. It's also adding toxic levels of vitamin D.

This fascinating book tells the whole story about milk. How it once was nature's perfect food...how "raw," unprocessed milk can heal and boost your immune system ... why you can't buy it legally in this country anymore, and what we could do to change that.

Dr. "Douglass traveled all over the world, tasting all kinds of milk from all kinds of cows, poring over dusty research books in ancient libraries far from home, to write this light-hearted but scientifically sound book.

The
Milk Book

William Campbell Douglass II, MD

Eat Your Cholesterol!

Eat Meat, Drink Milk, Spread The Butter- And Live Longer!
How to Live off the Fat of the Land and Feel Great.

Americans are being saturated with anti-cholesterol propaganda. If you watch very much television, you're probably one of the millions of Americans who now has a terminal case of cholesterol phobia. The propaganda is relentless and is often designed to produce fear and loathing of this worst of all food contaminants. You never hear the food propagandists bragging about their product being fluoride-free or aluminum-free, two of our truly serious food-additive problems. But cholesterol, an essential nutrient, not proven to be harmful in any quantity, is constantly pilloried as a menace to your health. If you don't use corn oil, Fleischmann's margarine, and Egg Beaters, you're going straight to atherosclerosis hell with stroke, heart attack, and premature aging -- and so are your kids. Never feel guilty about what you eat again! Dr. Douglass shows you why red meat, eggs, and dairy products aren't the dietary demons we're told they are. But beware: This scientifically sound report goes against all the "common wisdom" about the foods you should eat. Read with an open mind.

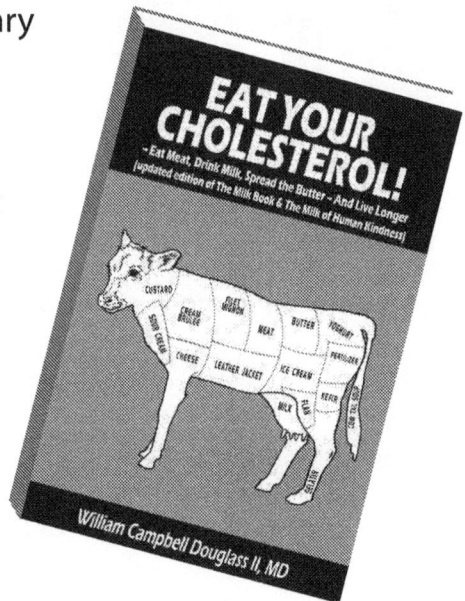

EAT YOUR CHOLESTEROL!
- Eat Meat, Drink Milk, Spread the Butter - And Live Longer
[updated edition of The Milk Book & The Milk of Human Kindness]

William Campbell Douglass II, MD

Rhino Publishing, S.A.
www.rhinopublish.com

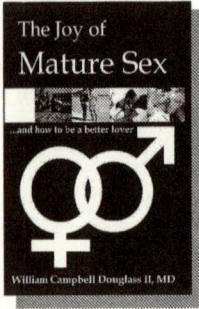

The Joy of Mature Sex and How to Be a Better Lover

Humans are very confused about what makes good sex. But I believe humans have more to offer each other than this total licentiousness common among animals. We're talking about mature sex. The kind of sex that made this country great.

Stop Aging or Slow the Process How Exercise With Oxygen Therapy (EWOT) Can Help

EWOT (pronounced ee-watt) stands for Exercise With Oxygen Therapy. This method of prolonging your life is so simple and you can do it at home at a minimal cost. When your cells don't get enough oxygen, they degenerate and die and so you degenerate and die. It's as simple as that.

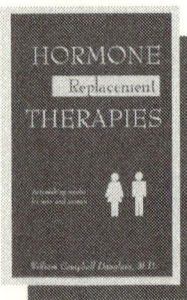

Hormone Replacement Therapies: Astonishing Results For Men And Women

It is accurate to say that when the endocrine glands start to fail, you start to die. We are facing a sea change in longevity and health in the elderly. Now, with the proper supplemental hormones, we can slow the aging process and, in many cases, reverse some of the signs and symptoms of aging.

Add 10 Years to Your Life With some "best of" Dr. Douglass' writings.

To add ten years to your life, you need to have the right attitude about health and an understanding of the health industry and what it's feeding you. Following the established line on many health issues could make you very sick or worse! Achieve dynamic health with this collection of some of the "best of" Dr. Douglass' newsletters.

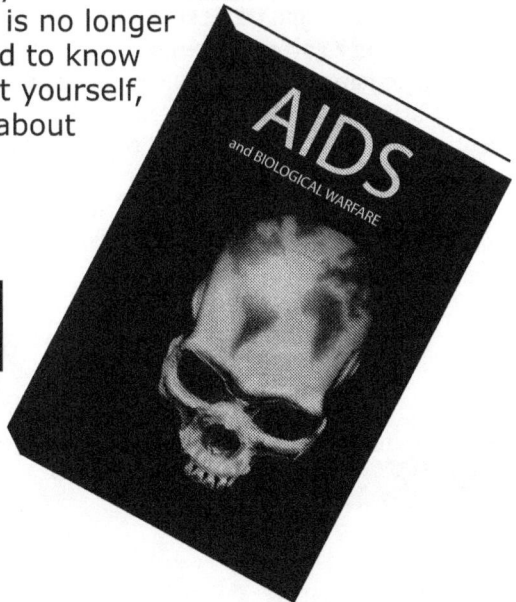

PAINFUL DILEMMA

Are we fighting the wrong war?

We are spending millions on the war against drugs while we
should be fighting the war against pain with those drugs!

As you will read in this book, the war on drugs was lost a long time ago and,
when it comes to the war against pain, pain is winning! An article in USA Today
(11/20/02) reveals that dying patients are not getting relief from pain. It seems
the doctors are torn between fear of the government, certainly justified, and a
clinging to old and out dated ideas about pain, which is NOT justified.

A group called Last Acts, a coalition of health-care groups, has released a very
discouraging study of all 50 states that nearly half of the 1.6 million Americans
living in nursing homes suffer from untreated pain. They said that life was being
extended but it amounted to little more than "extended pain and suffering."

This book offers insight into the history of pain treatment and the current failed
philosophies of contemporary medicine. Plus it describes some of today's most
advanced treatments for alleviating certain kinds of pain. This book is not another
"self-help" book touting home remedies; rather, Painful Dilemma: Patients in
Pain -- People in Prison, takes a hard look at where we've gone wrong and what
we (you) can do to help a loved one who is living with chronic pain.

The second half of this book is a must read if you value your freedom. We now
have the ridiculous and tragic situation of people
in pain living in a government-created hell by
restriction of narcotics and people in prison for
trying to bring pain relief by the selling of
narcotics to the suffering. The end result of the
"war on drugs" has been to create the greatest
and most destructive cartel in history, so great,
in fact, that the drug Mafia now controls most
of the world economy.

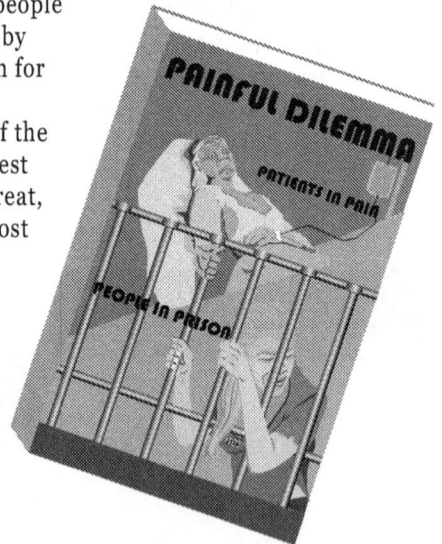

Live the Adventure!

Why would anyone in their right mind put everything they own in storage and move to Russia, of all places?! But when maverick physician Bill Douglass left a profitable medical practice in a peaceful mountaintop town to pursue "pure medical truth".... none of us who know him well was really surprised.

After All, anyone who's braved the outermost reaches of darkest Africa, the mean streets of Johannesburg and New York, and even a trip to Washington to testify before the Senate, wouldn't bat and eye at ducking behind the Iron Curtain for a little medical reconnaissance!

Enjoy this imaginative, funny, dedicated man's tales of wonder and woe as he treks through a year in St. Petersburg, working on a cure for the world's killer diseases. We promise --

YOU WON'T BE BORED!

Rhino Publishing S.A.
www.rhinopublish.com

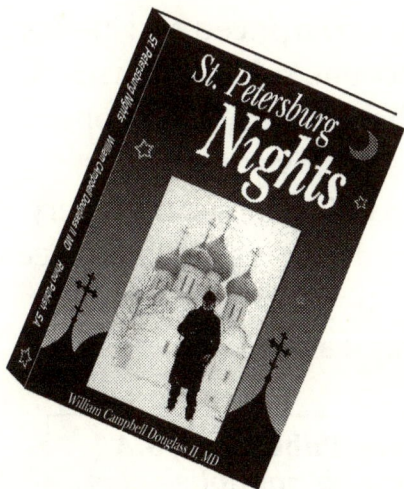

St. Petersburg Nights

William Campbell Douglass II, MD

THE SMOKER'S PARADOX
THE HEALTH BENEFITS OF TOBACCO!

The benefits of smoking tobacco have been common knowledge for centuries. From sharpening mental acuity to maintaining optimal weight, the relatively small risks of smoking have always been outweighed by the substantial improvement to mental and physical health. Hysterical attacks on tobacco notwithstanding, smokers always weigh the good against the bad and puff away or quit according to their personal preferences. Now the same anti-tobacco enterprise that has spent billions demonizing the pleasure of smoking is providing additional reasons to smoke. Alzheimer's, Parkinson's, Tourette's Syndrome, even schizophrenia and cocaine addiction are disorders that are alleviated by tobacco. Add in the still inconclusive indication that tobacco helps to prevent colon and prostate cancer and the endorsement for smoking tobacco by the medical establishment is good news for smokers and non-smokers alike. Of course the revelation that tobacco is good for you is ruined by the pharmaceutical industry's plan to substitute the natural and relatively inexpensive tobacco plant with their overpriced and ineffective nicotine substitutions. Still, when all is said and done, the positive revelations regarding tobacco are very good reasons indeed to keep lighting those cigars - but only 4 a day!

Rhino Publishing, S.A
www.rhinopublish.com

Bad Medicine
How Individuals Get Killed By Bad Medicine.

Do you really need that new prescription or that overnight stay in the hospital? In this report, Dr. Douglass reveals the common medical practices and misconceptions endangering your health. Best of all, he tells you the pointed (but very revealing!) questions your doctor prays you never ask. Interesting medical facts about popular remedies are revealed.

Dangerous Legal Drugs
The Poisons in Your Medicine Chest.

If you knew what we know about the most popular prescription and over-the-counter drugs, you'd be sick. That's why Dr. Douglass wrote this shocking report about the poisons in your medicine chest. He gives you the low-down on different categories of drugs. Everything from painkillers and cold remedies to tranquilizers and powerful cancer drugs.

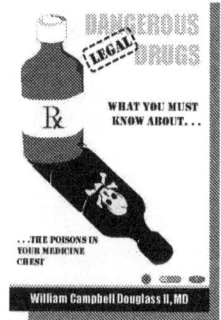

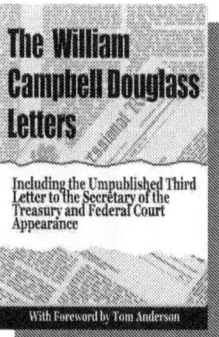

The William Campbell Douglass Letters.
Expose of Government Machinations
(Vietnam War).

THE WILLIAM CAMPBELL DOUGLASS LETTERS. Dr. Douglass' Defense in 1968 Tax Case and Expose of Government Machinations during the Vietnam War.

The Eagle's Feather. A Novel of
International Political Intrigue.

Although The Eagle's Feather is a work of fiction set in the 1970's, it is built, as with most fiction, on a framework of plausibility and background information. This is a fiction book that could not have been written were it not for various ominous aspects, which pose a clear and present danger to the security of the United States.

Rhino Publishing

ORDER FORM

PURCHASER INFORMATION

Purchaser's Name (Please Print): _____

Shipping Address (Do not use a P.O. Box): _____

City: _____ State/Prov.: _____ Country: _____

Zip/Postal Code: _____ Telephone No.: _____ Fax No.: _____

E-Mail Address (if interested in receiving free e-Books when available): _____

CREDIT CARD INFO (CIRCLE ONE):

MASTERCARD, VISA, AMERICAN EXPRESS, DISCOVER, JCB, DINER'S CLUB, CARTE BLANCHE.

Charge my Card -> Number #: _____ Exp.: _____

*Security Code: _____ * Required for all MasterCard, Visa and American Express purchases. For your security, we require that you enter your card's verification number. The verification number is also called a CCV number. This code is the 3 digits farthest right in the signature field on the back of your VISA/MC, or the 4 digits to the right on the front of your American Express card. Your credit card statement will show **a different name than Rhino Publishing** as the vendor.

WE DO NOT share your private information, we use 3rd party credit card processing service to process your order only.

ADDITIONAL INFORMATION

If your shipping address is not the same as your credit card billing address, please indicate your card billing address here.

_____   Type of card: _____

Name on the card

Billing Address: _____

City: _____   State/Prov.: _____   Zip/Postal Code: _____

Fax a copy of this order to:
RHINO PUBLISHING, S.A.
1-888-317-6767 or International #: + 416-352-5126

To order by mail, send your payment by first class mail only to the following address. Please include a copy of this order form. Make your check or bank drafts (NO postal money order) payable to RHINO PUBLISHING, S.A. and mail to:

Rhino Publishing, S.A.
Attention: PTY 5048
P.O. Box 025724
Miami, FL.
USA 33102

Digital E-books also available online: www.rhinopublish.com

Rhino Publishing

ORDER FORM

Purchaser's Name (Please Print): _____

I would like to order the following paperback book of Dr. Douglass (Alternative Medicine Books):

___ X	9962-636-04-3	Add 10 Years to Your Life. With some "best of" Dr. Douglass writings.	$13.99 $ ___
___ X	9962-636-07-8	AIDS and Biological Warfare. What They Are Not Telling You!	$17.99 $ ___
___ X	9962-636-09-4	Bad Medicine. How Individuals Get Killed By Bad Medicine.	$11.99 $ ___
___ X	9962-636-10-8	Color Me Healthy. The Healing Power of Colors.	$11.99 $ ___
___ X	9962-636 -XX-X	Color Filters for Color Me Healthy. 11 Basic Roscolene Filters for Lamps.	$21.89 $ ___
___ X	9962-636-15-9	Dangerous Legal Drugs. The Poisons in Your Medicine Chest.	$13.99 $ ___
___ X	9962-636-18-3	Dr. Douglass' Complete Guide to Better Vision. Improve eyesight naturally.	$11.99 $ ___
___ X	9962-636-19-1	Eat Your Cholesterol! How to Live off the Fat of the Land and Feel Great.	$11.99 $ ___
___ X	9962-636-12-4	Grandma Bell's A To Z Guide To Healing. Her Kitchen Cabinet Cures.	$14.99 $ ___
___ X	9962-636-22-1	Hormone Replacement Therapies. Astonishing Results For Men & Women	$11.99 $ ___
___ X	9962-636-25-6	Hydrogen Peroxide: One of the Most Underused Medical Miracle.	$15.99 $ ___
___ X	9962-636-27-2	Into the Light. New Edition with Blood Irradiation Instrument Instructions.	$19.99 $ ___
___ X	9962-636-54-X	Milk Book. The Classic on the Nutrition of Milk and How to Benefit from it.	$17.99 $ ___

__	X	9962-636-00-0	Painful Dilemma - Patients in Pain - People in Prison.	$17.99	$__
__	X	9962-636-32-9	Prostate Problems. Safe, Simple, Effective Relief for Men over 50.	$11.99	$__
__	X	9962-636-34-5	St. Petersburg Nights. Enlightening Story of Life and Science in Russia.	$17.99	$__
__	X	9962-636-37-X	Stop Aging or Slow the Process. Exercise With Oxygen Therapy Can Help.	$11.99	$__
__	X	9962-636-60-4	The Hypertension Report. Say Good Bye to High Blood Pressure.	$11.99	$__
__	X	9962-636-48-5	The Joy of Mature Sex and How to Be a Better Lover...	$13.99	$__
__	X	9962-636-43-4	The Smoker's Paradox: Health Benefits of Tobacco.	$14.99	$__

Political Books:

__	X	9962-636-40-X	The Eagle's Feather. A 70's Novel of International Political Intrigue.	$15.99	$__
__	X	9962-636-46-9	The W. C. D. Letters. Expose of Government Machinations (Vietnam War).	$11.99	$__

SUB-TOTAL: $__

	ADD $5.00 HANDLING FOR YOUR ORDER:	$ 5.00	$ 5.00
X	ADD $2.50 SHIPPING FOR EACH ITEM ON ORDER:	$ 2.50	$__
	NOTE THAT THE MINIMUM SHIPPING AND HANDLING IS $7.50 FOR 1 BOOK ($5.00 + $2.50) For order shipped outside the US, add $5.00 per item		
X	ADD $5.00 S. & H. OR EACH ITEM ON ORDER (INTERNATIONAL ORDERS ONLY)	$ 5.00	$__
__	Allow up to 21 days for delivery (we will call you about back orders if any)		

TOTAL: $__

Fax a copy of this order to: 1-888-317-6767 or Int'l + 416-352-5126
or mail to: Rhino Publishing, S.A. Attention: PTY 5048 P.O. Box 025724, Miami, FL., 33102 USA
Digital E-books also available online: www.rhinopublish.com

www.ingramcontent.com/pod-product-compliance
Lightning Source LLC
Chambersburg PA
CBHW032056040426
42335CB00036B/420